AGING WELL:
Exploring the Land of Our Later Years

AGING WELL

EXPLORING THE LAND OF
OUR LATER YEARS

Haley's
Athol, Massachusetts

Haley's
Post Office Box 248
Athol, Massachusetts 01331
1.800.215.8805

The names and identifying characteristics of the clients discussed in this book have been changed to preserve their privacy and to respect the confidentiality assured by the agencies for whom the author was volunteering as counselor or companion. Persons whose full names are given have approved the information about them included in this book.

Book and cover designs by Marcia Gagliardi.
Cover photograph by Helen Hills.
Copy edited by Dorothy E. Hayden.
Photographs by Marcia Gagliardi unless otherwise credited.
Printed by the Highland Press.

Library of Congress Cataloging-in-Publication Data
Hills, Helen R. W. 1929-
     Aging well : exploring the land of our later years / Helen Hills.
          p.   cm.
     Includes bibliographical references and index.
     ISBN 1-884540-35-X
     1. Aged--United States--Psychology. 2. Aged--United States--Life skills guides. 3. Depression in old age--United States. 4. Loneliness in old age--United States. 5. Happiness in old age--United States.
I. Title
HQ10645.U5H55   1998
305.26--dc21

                                                                          98-8652
                                                                          CIP

To my husband, Ralph,
whose unwavering belief in my mission and abilities
has supported both my commitment to the elderly
and my work on this book.

Contents

List of Illustrations

Foreword

When Helen Hills arrived in my office six years ago aspiring to become a volunteer companion for the elderly, her energy, intelligence, and desire to learn were immediately obvious to me. The same qualities, along with humor and compassion, come through clearly in her book.

Aging Well: Exploring the Land of Our Later Years is a guide for anyone in middle age looking toward the future with some trepidation as well as for those dealing with elders in their personal or professional lives. It should also serve as an incentive for volunteer work and a resource for those supervising volunteers.

As Helen's supervisor for several years, I learned from her clients how much they came to value her genuine interest in them. When she asked if I would like to see the notes she prepared on visits with them, I assented and was impressed with their detail and warmth. Besides, she is a very engaging writer.

I had, like Helen, been drawn to working with elders in part to learn about the next stage in life. I have now been with Franklin County Home Care for more than a decade, in close and frequent contact with individual elders. From personal experience, I can attest that Helen reports what she has observed with an unflinching gaze. Nevertheless, she finds much to offer hope. Her book will provide readers with an accurate and bright picture of what old age can be. Unlike some of the more scholarly texts on the subject, *Aging Well* is written in a down-to-earth and even jaunty style.

Helen emphasizes what I have come to believe is the most important ingredient in aging well: attitude. Her many stories and quotations show what it feels like to grow old and what helps or hinders the process. Her balanced discussion of the spiritual aspects of aging is especially inspiring.

Really, Helen herself is inspiring. The fact shines through everything she has written here.

—LINDA COMSTOCK

Licensed Certified Social Worker
Franklin County Home Care Corporation

Acknowledgments

First of all, I want to thank the unnamed clients with whom I have worked over the past six years. They deserve my thanks for their willingness to reveal their varied experiences of aging. I also want to thank the persons who graciously consented to be interviewed and photographed, as well as the members of the Horse Mountain Jazz Band, who supplied personal information and photographs.

The social workers who have provided supervision richly deserve mention. June Tomaso-Wood, continuing head of the Elder Peer Counselor progam in Franklin County, Massachusetts, initiated me to the world of the elderly, going out of her way to give me training at the time that I was ready for it, rather than at her own convenience. Linda Comstock soon after counseled me as a companion for the elderly in the Franklin County Home Care program. She was capably followed by Chris Baronas and then Patty MacDonald. The insights of all these professionals have contributed to my knowledge and skills.

Second to last but certainly not least, I want to express my appreciation to publisher Marcia Gagliardi, whose advice concerning both the content and form of this book have been invaluable. She helped me develop its regional and popular appeal without diminishing its original scholarly content, remaining patient, cheerful, and upbeat despite my occasional downbeats. But then there is no music without both the downbeats and the upbeats, is there?

The reference to music brings me to my musician husband, Ralph, who, never questioning my conviction that this book must be written, at times turned his back on his piano, flugelhorn, and euphonium to feed horses, dogs, and cats when it was supposed to have been *my* turn. And never complained if dinner was late or meager. What more can an author wish for!

Introduction

In aging we gain as well as lose. The autumn of human life, like the autumn of nature, can bring richness of beauty. It's a time when our spiritual forces seem to expand. A life of the heart and of the mind takes over while our physical force ebbs away.

[Polly Francis, *Songs*, p. 33]

This book is targeted primarily at those of us who are not yet old or just beginning to know that we are old. It points to the need to prepare for the very different and challenging years that lie ahead.

I have written this book as much for myself as for you. As I start along the path of my own later years, I am wondering what will lie ahead for me, just as you wonder what life will bring you. I know this will indeed be a time of discovery—but of exactly what I am not sure. To help me handle whatever challenges may lie ahead, I expect to read and reread parts of this book over the years. It contains wisdom from those who have been there, and thus it will be valuable as I enter further into the land of old age.

You might think that, having written this book, I would remember all that is in it. Not so. Being sixty-eight years old as I write, I know that most of the wonderful quotations it presents will have slipped from my memory. I will remember the many people whose experiences of aging are described here, but I may need to be reminded of their inspiring words and the examples, as well as the warnings, that their lives provide.

I am among those who are sometimes termed the "young old." I remain fully active but definitely not as energetic or physically able as I was ten years ago. I can still ride horseback for several hours, but my back creaks and complains if I ride longer. I can shepherd the dogs up forest trails at a fast pace for hours at a time, but I may have to puff and pause a moment—or perhaps two—at the crest of hills. And I have finally admitted that hiring someone to clean my house is not

The author starts out on her regular hike with her new dog, Sunny.

merely a luxury but a necessity if I am not to alternate between the back-breaking vacuum cleaner and my beloved heating pad.

Nevertheless, and this is the amazing thing to me, I have never felt more self-confident and creative. As my body begins to wear out here and there, I am aware of an increasing spiritual energy. If this were not so, why would I bother, at this time of my life, to expend the effort and time required to research and write this book?

After all, I have raised four children, spent fifteen years after my divorce earning a sufficiently good living to support not only myself but my animals, and finally found—not without effort—a new husband just right for me. This should be the time to rest, relax, and take up a new hobby.

At first, that seemed the natural thing to do. During the same year that I remarried at the age of sixty-one, I also retired from twenty-five years with the U.S. Department of Education and moved from suburban Maryland to rural Massachusetts. My husband and I brought with us my two horses, which I had previously kept at a stable and ridden only on weekends. Now I had the challenge and joy of keeping my horses on my own property and riding out with new friends on nearby trails whenever I wished.

It had vaguely occurred to me that once I had settled into our new house and worked out a routine, those pleasures just possibly might not be enough. How right that passing thought was. I found within the year that I had energy to spare and enough empty time to feel threatened with boredom and depression. Of course, I could have washed the floors or polished the furniture, but that possibility in itself drove me to look for something else to do. Besides, I had always regretted not having the time, while commuting to and from my job in Washington, D.C., to respond to volunteer causes.

In good health and only sixty-two, I was facing who knows how many years without the mind-engaging work for which my entire self yearned. And, aware of the fact that old age was approaching, I wondered what those years would be like. The solution was obvious to me. I could become a volunteer for agencies that help the elderly, thus satisfying my desire to be of service and also acquainting myself with what it is like to be old. Perhaps at the same time I would be banishing the threat of boredom and usefully harnessing my surplus energy.

For a close look at life over seventy, I contacted local agencies and under their sponsorship began visiting older people. First, I trained and earned status as an "elder peer counselor" in a Franklin County program that offers assistance to

Astride her Arabian gelding, Fahli, the author heads for the trail.

people over sixty-five who are trying to cope with a loss of some kind, such as a mate, a home, eyesight, or perhaps use of a car. A few months later, I joined the county's home care agency, which provides many services, including a weekly "companion." Because this position would give me the opportunity to meet more elderly people, I quickly volunteered as a companion.

And so, for the past six years, I have been spending the major part of three days each week going to the homes of people whom I have come to feel are my elderly friends. The most important part of my work for both programs was listening, and so I have personally heard the life stories, disappointments, concerns, and hopes of more than forty people over seventy years old. Most have been women, primarily because women tend to outlive men and thus are the ones most likely to live alone. Usually I found some combination of loneliness, boredom, and depression.

After a few more months, I became aware that I was not seeing the entire picture by a long shot. The people I visited were those who needed and sought some kind of aid from the county. But surely there were others out there who did not seek help. Did they have the same problems? Were their lives fuller and happier? And if so, why? In short, I needed a more comprehensive understanding of aging.

So, as a lifelong reader, I began to delve into the growing body of English-language literature on the subject, both fiction and nonfiction, mostly written by articulate, thoughtful, and sensitive people in their seventies, eighties, and nineties during the past hundred years or so. I did a lot of stimulating and rewarding research. I found not only problems similar to those of the elderly people I was visiting, but unexpected possibilities for growth and new joys in our later years.

It was precisely this discovery that sparked the idea of writing a book. I felt I simply had to share the treasures I had found with everyone who was aging or who was trying to help the elderly. I knew that most people would not have the opportunity or inclination to follow the time-consuming path I had taken, so I decided to condense into one convenient book what I had learned from hours and hours of visiting and reading. After ascertaining that no such book was already available, I set to work to fill the void.

I still had no live witnesses, however, to what it is like to age successfully. To fill that gap, I interviewed in person a number of people in their eighties who had clearly aged well. They were still living fulfilling and active lives. All whom I approached consented graciously to talk with me about their own experiences and so to help me understand what it takes to meet the challenges of old age. They also agreed to let me use their names.

This book is thus a brief introduction to what it is often like—and may sometimes be like—to be old, based largely on firsthand experiences. It begins by describing frankly but briefly the psychological challenges encountered in aging. For the fears, I have been able to give a bit of reassurance, and for the daily battle with loneliness, boredom, and depression, I have suggested concrete remedies and preventive actions. Next comes an encouraging section on the potential joys and rewards, as described by those who have aged well and chosen to write or talk to me about their experiences. Although the very beginning may leave a reader dreading the years beyond seventy-five or eighty, the discussion of the joys and rewards of later years may even arouse some anticipation.

Once the overall picture has been sketched with both its shadows and its lights, the next chapter describes how others have successfully met the challenges and reaped the rewards. It includes stories about the elderly people I have visited for the local agencies, what they have told me and what they have done. Their names and identifying characteristics have of course been changed to preserve their privacy. The stories of some elders from my immediate area who are still clearly enjoying their lives may be particularly appealing and helpful. There are also a host of quotations from the writings of many notable elderly people, each telling what growing old has been like for them, the difficulties they have faced and the wisdom they have gained. Although several authors write of similar experiences, their ways of viewing and describing them are so different that I decided not to eliminate quotations just to reduce their number. Most are vivid and concise. Some are humorous, still others are touching, and all have a message worth hearing. Each quotation may be the one that echoes a familiar feeling or speaks in your language.

The last chapter describes attitudes, approaches, and techniques I have found useful in my work with elderly persons. I hope it will help the many compassionate persons now trying to relieve the suffering of the elderly and perhaps freshen the approach of those with more experience in this work than I have. It may also provide a few useful hints for establishing a more interesting relationship with aging relatives and friends.

An annotated bibliography completes the book, listing the most accessible and relevant publications I found on the subject. Final pages provide full source information for quotations in the text, where an abbreviated form appears.

Finally, a caution about what this book is *not*. It is not a source of detailed information or advice on several subjects about which elders are correctly concerned, including health, finances, housing, and sources of aid; nor is it an anthology of works on aging. Many excellent books and articles have been written on aging that deal with these subjects, some of which are listed in the annotated bibliography.

Fears, Challenges, and Joys

There are both advantages and disadvantages in being very old. The disadvantages are obvious and uninteresting, and I shall say little about them. The advantages seem to me more interesting.

[Bertrand Russell at the age of ninety, *Oxford*, p. 367]

At the Start

As we begin to look at what old age may bring, a disclaimer of sorts is both appropriate and necessary. Not only does old age bring different things to different people, but we are told by those who are there that we cannot understand it until we have ourselves arrived. Poet Malcolm Cowley, writing at the age of eighty, warns

> To enter the country of old age is a new experience, different from what you supposed it to be. Nobody, man or woman, knows the country until he has lived in it and has taken out his citizenship papers.

[Cowley, pp. 2-3]

Mark Twain, speaking at a dinner when he was seventy, remarked that

> we can't reach old age by another man's road.

[Twain, *Oxford*, p. 303]

Florida Scott-Maxwell, author, activist, and psychologist, at eighty-three phrases the same idea this way.

> I want to tell people approaching and perhaps fearing age that it is a time of discovery. If they say—"Of what?" I can only answer, "We must find out for ourselves, otherwise it won't be discovery."

[Scott-Maxwell, p. 142]

Polly Francis, a fashion illustrator and photographer, wrote three famous articles on old age when she was between ninety-one and ninety-four. In her first article, entitled "The Autumn of My Aging," she expresses less pleasure in aging than Scott-Maxwell, but agrees that we cannot really know what it is until we ourselves age:

> What a baffling thing old age is! It doesn't bring the peace we were led to expect. I find it hard to drift with the stream; all along the way there are problems which obstruct the smooth flow of life. The area which lies between the "here" and the "hereafter" is a difficult passage to travel. One must make the journey to fully understand it.
>
> [Francis, *Songs*, p. 30]

Nevertheless, we can learn something about the path we all eventually travel from the reports of those who have walked it. A realistic overall statement about age is made by Eda LeShan, not yet from personal experience but from knowledge gained during interviews for her commonsense books and articles on aging.

> Old age, just exactly like every other stage of our lives, is full of ambiguities. What really bugs me about the "prime of your life" enthusiasts is not that they lie, but they settle for half-truths. There are those who *are* having "the time of their lives," but even for those there is the poignant ever-present background music of time running out. And for many— the chronically ill, the physically handicapped, the poor, the lonely—old age can be a disaster.
>
> [LeShan, *50 Again*, p. 17]

The editors of a fascinating anthology of literature on growing old, *Songs of Experience*, also note a combination of good and bad in their introduction:

> Our probing of the literature confirms that old age is definitely a time of supreme paradox. It can offer the greatest challenges and the most exquisite personal rewards.
>
> [Fowler and McCutcheon, *Songs*, xvi]

Similarly, the editors of another fine anthology, *The Oxford Book of Aging*, in the introduction to a chapter on the value of work in the later years, write of

> the paradox of physical decline and spiritual growth.
>
> [Cole and Winkler, *Oxford*, p. 183]

Much of what has been written about aging is upbeat, no doubt because we are all aware of the downbeat side and do not need to be reminded. I agree and have written accordingly. Observation of this paradox is hardly new. Plato commented that "the spiritual eyesight improves as the physical eyesight declines."

Disbelief

For all of us who have passed fifty-five, disbelief comes first. There was one day when we looked into the mirror or felt more than a twinge of pain in a joint and admitted to ourselves that—perhaps—we were "moving toward" old age, but of course we were not yet old. We feel that we are the same individuals we always were, only now looking a bit as if we are wearing some cosmetics to make us look elderly. I vividly remember meeting a college friend a number of years after we had graduated and being absolutely astounded at her appearance. She really did look as if she were wearing stage make-up, and I could not rid myself of the illusion that I could wipe it all away and reveal the same young woman I had known.

Francis, again in her first article about aging, writes of a slow change leading to a sudden realization.

Age creeps up so stealthily that it is often with shock that we become aware of its presence. Perhaps that is why so many of us reach old age utterly unprepared to meet its demands. We may be a bit rebellious about accepting it; I want to cry out that the invisible part of me is not old.

[Francis, *Songs*, p. 31]

Author Elizabeth Gray Vining describes similar feelings at the age of seventy.

It isn't as if I felt old. I don't. Inside I feel often as gauche, as shy, as incapable of wise or effective action as I did at sixteen, or as surprised and delighted by unexpected beauty. But in actual fact I shall be seventy on my birthday, which occurs in a little more than a month.

[Vining, p. 4]

Vining uses the metaphor of a door and a wall to help us glimpse the experience of knowing that we are really approaching the end of life.

A door shuts. It is shut not in one's face but behind one. In front is a new landscape, bleak perhaps at times, lit no doubt at others with mysterious beauty, but cut off in the distance by a wall, which for the first time is close enough to be visible. One stands in a limited space, with the door behind and the wall somewhere in front.

[Vining, pp. 4-5]

Maurice Goudeket, husband of the French novelist and essayist Colette, in *The Delights of Growing Old*, asks other seventy-five-year-olds,

Has the "me" of your first adult years changed in any way? There is shortness of breath, a slowness of movement, a back that will not bend so easily, to be sure, but these are things for our bodies to cope with. The immaterial being that gives our threatened building all its life does not show a single wrinkle, nor will it ever do so.

[Goudeket, p. 4]

Goudeket's response to the number of his years is astonishment, as well as disbelief.

Beatrice Wood, a ninety-year-old artist, expresses this surprise most amusingly.

I looked in the mirror the other morning and I said, "Oh, there's a horse. I look like a horse." Well, what of it? I do look like a horse. But then I have fun making up and combing my hair, and then it doesn't bother me anymore that I'm old. I can't tell you why.

[Wood, *Ageless*, p. 278]

Wood continues in the same humorous vein when she claims that, despite being an "old crock," she is really only a teenager.

There's no question that the outside of an individual does change and wither and wrinkle, but very curiously the inside does not change and you will hear ever so many people say that. Even if they are old crocks, they will say, "I don't feel old." . . . I know I'm ninety because people tell me I'm ninety. Inwardly, I just laugh because, inwardly, I'm not in my nineties. I'm still sixteen or seventeen. And I have a very good time.

[Wood, *Ageless*, pp. 279-80]

Assuming basic good health, tiring more easily than before follows a changing appearance as one of the earlier signs of aging. This is well described by author M. F. K. Fisher in her seventy-seventh year.

I seem almost unconsciously, or perhaps only will-nilly, to be winding down. It is like being a wound clock: I have the original mechanism, but the ticking is slower, and some of the intricate tiny artful gears have worn down with long usage, so that now and then the ticking may falter.

[Fisher, *Last House*, p. 175]

Malcolm Cowley, writing at eighty years of age, stages a recognizable scene.

The new octogenarian feels as strong as ever when he is sitting back in a comfortable chair. . . . It seems to him that old age is only a costume assumed for those others; the true, the essential self is ageless. In a moment he will rise and go for a ramble in the woods, taking a gun along, or a fishing rod, if it is spring. Then he creaks to his feet, bending forward to keep his balance, and realizes that he will do nothing of the sort. The body and its surroundings have their messages for him or only one message: "You are old."

[Cowley, p. 3]

The author's mirrors reflect her distress at sags and wrinkles.

On the same subject, Cowley wrote that

we start by growing old in other people's eyes, then slowly we come to share their judgment.

[Cowley, p.5]

In a series of vignettes in his poem "The Red Wagon," Malcolm Cowley describes the increasing pace of time as we age.

The Red Wagon

For his birthday they gave him a red express wagon
with a driver's high seat and a handle that steered.
His mother pulled him around the yard.
"Giddyap," he said, but she laughed and went off
to wash the breakfast dishes.

"I wanta ride too," his sister said,
and he pulled her to the edge of a hill.
"Now, sister, go home and wait for me,
but first give a push to the wagon."

He climbed again to the high seat,
this time grasping the handle-that-steered.
The red wagon rolled slowly down the slope,
then faster as it passed the schoolhouse
and faster as it passed the store,
the road still dropping away.
Oh, it was fun.

But would it ever stop?
Would the road always go downhill?

The red wagon rolled faster.
Now it was in strange country.
It passed a white house he must have dreamed about,
deep woods he had never seen,
a graveyard where, something told him, his sister was buried.

Far below
the sun was sinking into a broad plain.

The red wagon rolled faster.
Now he was clutching the seat, not even trying to steer.
Sweat clouded his heavy spectacles.
His white hair streamed in the wind.

[Cowley, pp. 6-7]

Frustration

Disbelief is followed by frustration at the changes that keep occurring as the years go by. Many persons are annoyed by a combination of sleeplessness at night and then sleepiness during the day, particularly the early evening. Science writer Dr. Christopher Hallowell explains that this is a normal occurrence, because

> after sixty, the circadian rhythm that makes younger people feel sleepy at night and permits them to sleep the night through begins to falter.
>
> [Hallowell, p. 53]

Since the change is physical, the only answer is to adapt to the inevitable.

Frustration occurs when we find that, even for those of us who are in "good shape," we have to limit the length of time we can do hard, physical work. And not only are the heart and lungs wearing out a bit, but sometimes other parts as well. The need to use eye glasses is one of the first frustrations, often coming well before the age of fifty. I continue to be annoyed every time I try to read something without my glasses—even after needing them all these years. And then perhaps hearing ability is diminished and we have to resort to a hearing aid. Not to mention the beginning of arthritis one place or another that can limit our range of activities.

And for those who are really frail or ill, frustration can reach its heights. During a long, debilitating illness in her seventy-ninth year, May Sarton, poet, novelist, and journalist, cried out,

> There's nothing right now that makes me unhappy in the old ways, when I was unhappily in love, or when someone died suddenly. So I said, "It's not grief that makes me cry, but frailty." This is true, because it's when I can't do something that I very much want to do that I find myself in tears. Sometimes it's a kind of shame for having so little strength, having to measure if I cross the room whether I have the strength to do it.
>
> [Sarton, *Endgame*, p. 313]

To many people, memory losses are the most disturbing as well as frustrating. These creep up on us, usually beginning with the inability to remember a name. Next it is where we have put something or what we came upstairs to do. So far, we can claim that we always had these difficulties. But then comes an unsuccessful search for a word that was on our lips and just disappeared. And another search, until we realize that something in our brains is not working as it always did. This can be the beginning of one of the many fears that cause so much distress, particularly for those of us who are just getting accustomed to the idea that we ourselves have begun to be old. It is happening to us.

Four Fears

Once we acknowledge that we are in fact aging, the four major fears that most of us experience concern loss—of mental powers, of independence, of our home or apartment, and finally of life, perhaps in that order of concern. We are afraid of becoming "senile," of becoming dependent on others, of being "put" in a nursing home, and finally of the act of dying (maybe in protracted agony and without dignity). Every one of the older people I have visited has voiced these fears, usually explicitly. I was pleased to find some reassurance on all four fronts that should allay our fears somewhat. In short, the percentages are in our favor.

Dr. Walter M. Bortz II, a leading authority on aging and author of *We Live Too Short and Die Too Long*, published in 1991, believes that

> the fear of being old and infirm is what keeps us from being old and healthy.
>
> [Bortz, p.2]

Dementia

Today, our fear of losing our mental powers generally focuses on Alzheimer's disease, a form of what is termed "dementia." Another major and familiar cause of dementia is a stroke. Every old person I have counseled or visited expresses fear of Alzheimer's disease, sometimes amusingly mispronouncing it as "old timers' disease." Dr. Christopher Hallowell, in his 1985 book, *Growing Old, Staying Young*, reassures us that aging and loss of mental functioning need not go together and that our fear may itself be contributing to some loss. Dr. Hallowell writes,

> Dementia is not, contrary to popular belief, a normal part of aging. In fact, most elderly people who are tested show little decline in cognitive function beyond minor forgetfulness. But they may be so brainwashed into thinking that age and mental fuzziness go together that they let their mental abilities and alertness decline.
>
> [Hallowell, p. 208]

He reports,

> A longitudinal study begun twenty-one years ago on aging and the mental capacities of 3,000 people in Seattle aged twenty-two to eighty-one years old found that mental abilities usually begin to decline between ages sixty-seven and seventy-four. . . . But typically, it was only the post-eighty group that exhibited mental abilities that were below the middle range of mental performance of young adults.
>
> [Hallowell, p. 52]

However, even this decline has been debated recently. In the September-October 1996 issue of *Harvard Magazine*, John Lauerman writes that research by two associate professors at Harvard Medical School, Marilyn Albert, a Massachusetts General Hospital neuropsychologist, and Dr. Frank Duffy, a Children's Hospital neurologist, . . . showed that—at least in healthy adults—brain activity [in the elderly] does not slow down, but rather speeds up.

[Lauerman, p. 61]

Lauerman explains this surprising fact by pointing out that there has been some natural selection by the eighties and nineties. He quotes Dr. Tom Perls, gerontologist at Beth Israel Hospital and director of geriatrics curriculum development at Harvard Medical School.

"But I think there's a demographic selection, a 'survival-of-the-fittest' phenomenon in deciding who lives into old age. For instance, you find that on average, men in their 90s are more likely to be cognitively intact than men in their 80s. People who have lost their cognitive capacity can't make the cut; you have to be extremely smart and assertive to live to be 100."

[Lauerman, p. 61]

Discussing the biology of the brain, Dr. Bortz points out the following five facts.

- The brain is an intensely complex and ever developing organism.
- People need not experience cognitive loss with age.
- Not every area of the intellect is involved when loss does occur.
- Such loss is very often the result of disuse and disease rather than aging.
- Exercise and use seem to influence brain function in a positive way.

[Bortz, p. 179]

Concerning Alzheimer's disease itself, he writes,

Alzheimer's disease is not aging. It is a disease. Most people, most old people, never get it. It is neither natural nor normal, and it certainly is not inevitable. We are due for a great societal awakening. We must no longer allow the image of a disease like AD to remain such a formidable presence as to color our sense of our own futures.

[Bortz, p. 99]

However, while maintaining that Alzheimer's disease is exactly that, a disease and not a necessary part of aging, Dr. Bortz does not minimize the seriousness or prevalence of it:

We have estimates that of every 100 persons living past the age of 74, a statistical 2.4 will contract the disease every year. This is about the same as for heart attacks. Forty-eight percent of persons over the age of 85 show some evidence of Alzheimer's disease. It is the fourth leading cause of death for people over age 65, killing 100,000 persons per year.

Most persons in nursing homes are there because of Alzheimer's disease.

[Bortz, p. 93]

Dr. Bortz is a leading advocate of increased research to combat the disease.

Dependence

Dr. Hallowell lays out reassuring facts about the probability that we will become in some way dependent. Of people over seventy-five, he writes that chronic diseases affect only half and force only twenty-two percent to alter their lives to some extent. However, of people eighty-five and older, thirty-five percent

> need some kind of assistance, whether it be help in walking, bathing, or eating.
>
> [Hallowell, p. 271]

Note that the last statement also means that sixty-five percent of those eighty-five years and older need *no* assistance.

Cowley, the author of the poem about the red wagon, paints disturbing pictures of what he calls

> a sharper fear, seldom discussed, that troubles many more old persons and sometimes leads to suicide. . . . Obviously, the fear is not of death; it is of becoming helpless. It is the fear of being as dependent as a young child, while not being loved as a child is loved, but merely being kept alive against one's will. It is the fear of having to be dressed by a nurse, fed by a nurse, kept quiet with tranquilizers (as babies with pacifiers), and of ringing (or not being able to ring) for a nurse to change one's sheets after soiling the bed.
>
> [Cowley, pp. 56-57]

Scott-Maxwell writes that, before an operation,

> I had one fear. What if something went wrong, and I became an invalid? What if I became a burden, ceased to be a person and became a problem, a patient, someone who could not die?
>
> [Scott-Maxwell, p. 91]

Although only in her sixties at the time of writing, Eda LeShan agrees and makes a telling point about how our expectations for complete recovery change.

> When I was younger, even though I may have railed against being sick, I knew deep down I would get well. Now each illness seems another part of general deterioration. It is, I think, my far greater awareness of mortality, and my fear of becoming dependent on the care of others.
>
> [LeShan, *50 Again,* p. 130]

Obviously, the longer we can maintain independence—financial, emotional, and physical—the happier we are. After all, independence is something that most people have striven to gain from childhood on through adolescence, and in the middle years it has often been attained, but only through hard work, persistence, and sometimes luck. This is particularly true for women. To have to surrender this hard-won status seems most unfair. However, full independence is often not possible to retain because of high living costs, loneliness that often comes with a mate's death, and physical weakness and disability in advanced years.

One of the greatest challenges, after struggling to retain independence as long as possible, is to let go, to learn to accept graciously whatever type and extent of dependence becomes necessary. We can only let go, however, if we have learned that our independence is not the source of our value. This is difficult, because our feeling of self worth is usually closely associated with the independence gained over the years.

May Sarton's journals vividly describe the tortuous voyage of a very independent writer from her decision to live completely by herself in an unfamiliar setting through her long struggle to accept the help she needed from many people. In one of her last journals, she writes,

> We are so bereft of pride and of the ability to stand up, shall we say, and we become more and more dependent. One of the things I am learning, and I am beginning to learn it better, is to accept being dependent.

[Sarton, *Encore*, p. 249]

In her novel, *Kinds of Love*, Sarton voices the frustration of aging in the musings of Christina, followed by her vision of how it would be to relax into dependence.

> "It can't be easy," Christina murmured. For this was, without doubt, the real ordeal of very old age—consciousness without power, the cruel truth about life, that we suffer most from seeing without being able to do, carried to the highest magnitude.
>
> "It was hard when I struggled against such dependence, and against being babied. Then one day I just gave up—gave up the ghost, you might say—just decided to rest on the strong arms God has provided."

[Sarton, *Kinds of Love*, pp. 256-57]

The problem is when to accept dependence and how much to accept. Cowley writes of giving up as a temptation.

> Not whiskey or cooking sherry but simply giving up is the greatest temptation of age. It is something different from a stoical acceptance of infirmities, which is something to be admired.

[Cowley, p. 14]

> The givers-up see no reason for working. Sometimes they lie in bed all day when moving about would still be possible, if difficult.

[Cowley, p. 15]

Gerontologists share consensus, expressed concisely by B. F. Skinner, professor emeritus of psychology at Harvard University.

> Helping really helps only those who need to be helped. Others are deprived of the chance to be active.

[Skinner, p. 82]

16

In other words, the advice we receive is to struggle as hard as we can to retain independence, but to face the inevitable increase of dependency bit by bit, and with good grace. Not easy, but one of the possible rewards of aging, as discussed below, is the hard-gained comfortable acquaintance with the self that allows one to relinquish independence as it becomes necessary.

Nursing Homes

Fear of dependence often focuses on nursing homes. One person I interviewed commented that it was her brief stay in a nursing home to recuperate following an operation that made her suddenly know she was old. She said she felt "diminished" by the experience. She felt so helpless, so like a baby. She had not been afraid of being temporarily in a nursing home, but the experience of dependence there—not avoidable because she was indeed dependent—hurt her spirit. After returning home, it took her many months to recover her self-confidence, her knowledge of who she was.

Most of the old people I visit have expressed a horror at the idea of ever going into a nursing home—any nursing home. Some even refuse to visit their friends who have had to do so. While sharing to some extent their fear, I worry about the strength of their aversion, because certainly some of them will have to go to a nursing home one day, either briefly to recuperate from a hospitalization, or for the rest of their lives. Betty Friedan reassures us, however, that

> only 5 percent of Americans over sixty-five are, in fact, in nursing homes, and less than 10 percent ever will be.
>
> [Friedan, *Fountain,* p. 22]

Scott-Maxwell, whose fear of dependence we noted earlier, describes the humiliating lack of independence that she expected at a nursing home.

> Being ill in a nursing home became my next task, a somber dance in which I knew some of the steps. I must conform. I must be correct. I must be meek, obedient, and grateful, on no account must I be surprising. If I deviated by the breadth of a toothbrush I would be in the wrong.
>
> [Scott-Maxwell, p. 91]

The situation is described as much worse than envisioned by Scott-Maxwell in the nursing home of Sarton's novel, *As We Are Now.* Written in 1973, the book is based on a real nursing home in New Hampshire where an old farmer who worked for Sarton was taken in his very old age. It was a place of cruelty and humiliation. *As We Are Now* is the novel that first drew my attention to the loneliness and needs of the elderly. Although it is powerful and absorbing, I do not recommend this book to anyone for whom a nursing home is an imminent possibility. But I do think it would be helpful to anyone who wants to understand the vulnerability of old age with a mind to providing some aid to the elderly.

Dr. Hallowell quotes Dr. Gardner Moment, a gerontologist at the National Institute's Gerontology Research Center, on the desire of gerontologists that the elderly lead active lives up until the end, adding that this is what most of the elderly wish also.

> "Gerontologists want people to live the best they can and then go puff at the end rather than into a nursing home." Most people want to do just this. They want to live long lives, but only if they can remain healthy until they die. Mental and/or physical incapacitation is more frightening than death itself.
>
> [Hallowell, p. 273]

Buckley Nursing Home in Greenfield, Massachusetts, houses more than a hundred residents, many of whom are involved in staff-assisted activities.

He adds an encouraging note, assuring us that

the prospects have never been brighter to live to a much greater age than we now do and suddenly die, go 'puff,' rather than to suffer a lingering death.

[Hallowell, p. 273]

Although my knowledge of nursing homes is not broad, I have visited many of their residents in my region of north central Massachusetts. In doing so, I have learned that the homes differ greatly in quality, size, and programs. Some aspects of quality are measurable and easily discovered. These include the number of staff per resident, access and frequency of medical care, and financial status. Other aspects require an attentive visit.

As I enter a nursing home, I sniff. The most obvious sign of high quality is delivered when my nose registers zero for urine odor, indicating that the staff have regularly spent a lot of time keeping the many incontinent residents and their rooms clean. Even the best nursing homes do not smell like a rose every time I open the door.

Moving into the foyer, I assess the courtesy and friendliness of the staff, both to me and to residents. Do I have to stand and wait at the main desk before the person on duty offers to help me? Does the nurse's aide greet the lady moving slowly along in the wheelchair or does she slip hurriedly past her? What is the practice for handling the old man who is shrieking that he wants to go home?

Once in the room of the friend I am visiting, I try to assess how she feels about the nursing home. Complaints about food I hear but pretty much ignore, knowing the difficulty of preparing taste-tempting institutional food. I do note that the best nursing homes individualize menus to meet each resident's dietary needs. Most particularly, I listen carefully to detect whether my friend dares to complain about any of the staff. Nursing homes in Franklin County have ombudsmen who visit each resident regularly for the specific purpose of hearing complaints and negotiating any necessary improvements with the nursing home's management. Nevertheless, some residents fear reprisal if they make any negative comments. For they are helpless, completely dependent on the good will of the staff.

I have sometimes wondered if I, self-confident as I am in many ways, might agree with Scott-Maxwell and decide to become "meek, obedient, and grateful." While discovering the quality of a nursing home is important, the size and type of programs offered should not be ignored. Some large nursing homes have many programs with an activities director. Programs range from social gatherings like sing-alongs to more individual pursuits like crafts. The smaller nursing homes usually offer fewer activities but because of their limited size can seem more like home. People's tastes and needs differ.

Resident Doris Dahl offers Susan Lahoski, recreation director, pointers on crocheting at Buckley Nursing Home.

It is important that the nursing home be appropriate for the individual. This is not always possible, because space may be unavailable in a particular nursing home at the specific moment that it is needed. However, if a long stay appears inevitable, moving to a nursing home suited to the individual should certainly be planned. Many books offer sound advice on choosing a nursing home, including several in the annotated bibliography.

Although very aware of the risks and fears experienced by the elderly as they enter a nursing home, I have found that this step may actually increase the joy—or decrease the pain—of living for some people. Having read Sarton's *As We Are Now* and heard so many fears expressed by elderly people, I was surprised. Of course there is the advantage of regular healthful food and personal care, but there are other less tangible benefits. My observation is based on the experiences of several friends and on a book by Tracy Kidder, *Old Friends*.

The most striking example of a woman whose quality of life was distinctly improved is Sally. She was only seventy years old when I first visited her in her neat second-floor apartment. Her entire right side had been paralyzed by a stroke. She could get around her apartment by holding onto the furniture, but she could not write, comb her hair, or dress herself. Unable to go down the stairs, she sat all day and sometimes all night in a chair by the window.

Sally claimed to have lost contact with everyone outside her family, and indeed that seemed to be true. Her only, and infrequent, visitors apart from her daughter were staff from social service agencies. Her daughter, however, stopped by almost every day for just a few minutes. The daughter had once worked as a cleaning woman in a hospital's gerontology section, and she vowed that her mother would never be subjected to incarceration with a bunch of "old crazy people."

Sally was very lonely in her apartment. I stopped by once a week and played simple board games with her, which she thoroughly enjoyed even though she had some mental damage and could not play any game well. Although she was usually in very low spirits when I arrived, saying she only wanted to die, it was easy to get her to laugh and smile.

Then Sally had another stroke and went to a hospital. I lost track of her when she moved for rehabilitation to another institution. Later, while visiting a friend who had entered a nursing home, I felt someone put a hand on my arm and say slowly, "I know you." It was Sally, and we were both absolutely delighted to see each other again.

I hardly recognized her. Her face had filled out, her hair was neatly curled, and she seemed to smile all the time. An important cause of the smile was a companionable roommate, a woman of eighty-eight who was more mobile than she, and with whom she could talk and share her minor complaints. She is clearly much happier than she had been when she was tucked away in the privacy of her little apartment.

Sally's experience is obviously not shared by everyone. More common are the mixed responses of Jean and Gertrude, both of whom are mentally competent.

Jean is a peppery little woman who was living alone in a middle-class home. I began visiting her after both her husband and her best friend had died, one after the other. She thoroughly enjoyed "lunching" weekly with me at just about every restaurant in the area that was open on Tuesdays. She particularly enjoyed eating at the town diner, where she met old acquaintances. Then, at the age of eighty-seven, she was diagnosed with cancer. After hospitalization, she went into the small nursing home of her choice. She had hoped to return home, but she broke her hip and so was condemned to stay longer in the nursing home.

Recovering from the long, painful period of recuperation, Jean is quietly resigned to her fate. She sits in her chair all day, reading and dozing. Her only friends are the kind staff, and her only other occasional visitors are her niece and a former volunteer from the home care agency. She says, with an air of contentment, "I am as happy as I can expect to be under the circumstances," meaning her age and the necessity of living in a nursing home. For Jean, the small nursing home she chose has become a real home, and she feels cared for by friends.

Gertrude is a large, independent German woman who also was living alone, in a first-floor apartment from which she could venture a bit, but only with help, to see a few old friends in the complex. Visiting friends gave her great pleasure. At ninety, she used a walker and was especially careful when we went out visiting.

One day, however, she fell in her apartment, was hospitalized, and entered a large nursing home. After initial pleasure at the food and company, she went into a period of great distress at the prospect of not returning home and no longer having her precious possessions with her. She would cry easily when I visited. However, after a while, I would find her smilingly engaged in any number of activities available at this nursing home—exercise circles, story telling, music recitals.

Although the staff encouraged me to interrupt Gertrude's activities when I arrived, I never did so. Instead, I left evidence that I had been there so she would know I had not forgotten her. She still tends to cry a bit when we talk, but not in the same way as before. She knows quite a few people, complains about those with dementia, and is altogether much engaged with what is going on. She is not dependent on me or her two other visitors—a nephew and an old friend who makes any purchases she may want. I am not sure that she is happier than she was before her fall, but she too is resigned in her own way, and in the nursing home she is able to have the companionship she enjoys.

The book that changed my thinking about nursing homes is *Old Friends*, written by Tracy Kidder and published in 1993. It begins with a quote from *Women of Trachis*, by Sophocles.

> There is an ancient proverb:
> Don't judge a life good or bad before it ends.

Reading this book taught me that, contrary to much popular thought, there can be life in a nursing home. Many people fear nursing homes because they seem to think that living in any meaningful way abruptly ends as one walks through the door. It is often seen as a holding pen where one awaits death, often hoping that it comes soon.

Tracy Kidder tells the story of real people in a real nursing home, focusing on two men who roomed together and became "old friends." Treating them all as the individual people that they are, he describes the different experiences of nursing home residents, facing old age and death in their own individual ways. He sees the nursing home as just another stage where we continue to play out our lives and to develop, each in our fashion. I recommend this book to anyone visiting residents of a nursing home or facing entrance into one.

An article, written as if by an aged former teacher of English confined to a wheelchair in a nursing home, suggests that there may still be plenty of life to live if you have learned how to do it. Listen to a few of her defiant remarks:

I may be old, but I'm not dead.

Perhaps you are surprised to hear this. You may be surprised to learn that people like me are still capable of original ideas, intelligent insights, and intense feelings. Passionate love affairs, for example, are not uncommon here. Pacemakers cannot regulate the wild, unbridled yearnings of the heart.

[Smith, "The Happy Memories Club," *The Atlantic Monthly*, December 1995, p. 108]

She then tells about her love affair with an aging historian, whom she calls "the joy of my life" and with whom she eventually must play a sort of affectionate game because of his second and disorienting stroke. This article did not surprise me, because I knew firsthand of a love affair in a nursing home between a handsome but blind older woman and an aging man, also a resident. I would almost always see them holding hands as they sat waiting in the corridor for medicine or a scheduled activity. Their faces shone with an unmistakable joy, and in her "sharing" group she spoke glowingly of her new relationship.

And yet more often there is the bittersweet truth that Francis pointed out from her nursing home room.

Our greatest need is not met. It is one that we never outgrow. It is the need to feel cherished by someone—to know that there is a place where we "belong." This is something that no retirement home, nursing home or hospital can provide. These institutions are staffed by dedicated people, but it is not their function to soothe our yearning hearts. The emotional strain would be too heavy.

[Francis, *Songs*, p. 31]

Vining, visiting friends in a nursing home, wrote of their need to talk to someone who would really listen.

All three of those whom I met, each so different from the others, had one thing in common: they needed desperately to talk. This is the real loneliness of old age—to be surrounded by people and yet not to have anyone to hear and respond. For myself I found the day strangely tiring.

[Vining, p. 122]

Because she herself was planning to move into a retirement community equipped with a nursing section, Vining discussed the pros and cons of giving up independent living in an apartment. She mentioned the very positive experience of one friend, which she attributed to that friend's character.

In the afternoon Eliza Foulke, an eighty-two-year-old friend happily tucked away in the Quaker retirement center, Foulkeways, told me that what old people want is security, privacy, and independence—and independence not least of the three. By independence she meant "not being told what to do." Surely love is needed too. But Eliza gives so much love that she would not think to mention it.

[Vining, p. 13]

Staff and residents prepare pots of pansies to decorate bay windows of Buckley Nursing Home. From left, Viola Bonzek, resident; Janet Stevens, recreation assistant, and Juliette Demers, resident.

Of another friend not in a nursing home, she wrote,

> She buys freedom at the price of loneliness and finds it a bargain.
>
> [Vining, p. 34]

For herself, Vining remained unsure about her move, and in an effort to make a decision made this analysis.

> There are two basically different ways of approaching what is so mincingly called the Later Years: the stick-it-out-in-the-world policy and the duck-into-safety policy. The first one sounds so much more gallant, the second slightly craven.
>
> If you have a family, sons and daughters or devoted nieces and nephews, to step in and take responsibility if you fall in the bathroom and break your hip, then you can afford to live dangerously. If you are, as I am, entirely alone, I think you at least examine carefully the second alternative.
>
> [Vining, p. 29]

It should be pointed out here that there are many intermediate steps between completely independent living and a nursing home. Possibilities differ by region, but usually they consist of retirement communities, congregate housing, retirement homes, adult family care, and rest homes. Vining, by the end of the journal of her seventieth year, has decided to make the move to a retirement community called Kendal. She makes this amusing observation.

> As I look forward to Kendal—and I do—I sometimes catch myself thinking of all the nice things I am going to do for those old people there, and then I remember that I am one of those old people myself. I don't think I want anybody doing kindly things for me.
>
> [Vining, p. 187]

Dying

Fear of death is the final and familiar fear, experienced off and on from childhood. It is a fear of becoming nothing, quite inconceivable to our minds. Philip Larkin expresses the thought in his poem *Aubade*, the first two stanzas of which are cited.

Aubade

I work all day, and get half-drunk at night.
Waking at four to soundless dark, I stare.
In time the curtain-edges will grow light.
Till then I see what's really always there:
Unresting death, a whole day nearer now,
Making all thought impossible but how
And where and when I shall myself die.
Arid interrogation: yet the dread
Of dying, and being dead,
Flashes afresh to hold and horrify.

The mind blanks at the glare. Not in remorse
—The good not done, the love not given, time
Torn off unused—nor wretchedly because
An only life can take so long to climb
Clear of its wrong beginnings, and may never;
But at the total emptiness for ever,
The sure extinction that we travel to
And shall be lost in always. Not to be here,
Not to be anywhere,
And soon; nothing more terrible, nothing more true.

[Larkin, *Songs*, pp. 340-41]

As with anything so central to mankind, humor enters to express and lighten our emotions about death. These days, small books of amusing remarks about death abound. The following samples, quoted by Dr. Bortz, express universal feelings.

I am not afraid of dying—I just don't want to be there when it happens.

[Woody Allen, quoted in Bortz, p. 245]

I do not wish to obtain immortality through my work. I wish to obtain it through not dying.

[Allen, quoted in Bortz, p. 254]

I know everybody has to die sooner or later, but I thought an exception would be made in my case.

[William Saroyan, quoted in Bortz, p. 254]

Most older people I have visited, however, seem to fear death itself very little, as corroborated by many authors. Malcolm Cowley wrote,

> Like many old people—or so it would seem from various reports—I think less about death than might be expected. As death comes nearer, it becomes less frightening, less a disaster, more an everyday fact to be noted and filed away.
>
> [Cowley, p. 29]

Wendell Berry, in the novel *The Memory of Old Jack*, tells how a ninety-two-year-old farmer thinks of death:

> He has no fear of death. It is coming, there is nothing to be done about it, and so he does not think about it much. It is the unknown, and he has come to the unknown before. Sometimes it has been very satisfying, the unknown. Sometimes not. Anyhow, what would a man his age propose to do instead of die? He has been around long enough to know that death is the only perfect cure for what ails mortals. After you have stood enough, you die, and that is all right.
>
> And so he does not think of death more often than necessary, and he can quit thinking about it any time he wants to. He does not think of what lies ahead. He will leave that to the Old Marster.
>
> [Berry, p. 30]

Vining at seventy also has little concern about death.

> It is there, ahead, but I don't think about it every day. It floats into my mind from time to time, awakened by a reference in a book, the death or serious illness of a friend, or just suddenly appearing out of nothing. . . . I don't fear death, but I do fear a protracted and painful dying.
>
> [Vining, pp. 91-92]

Thinking about death may even have an advantage, according to Cowley, who provides a vivid image from John Cowper Powys to make his point.

> The thought of death is never far absent, but it comes to be simply accepted. Often it is less a fear than a stimulus to more intense living. John Cowper Powys says, " . . . we poor dullards of habit and custom, we besotted and befuddled takers of life for granted, require the hell of a flaming thunderbolt to rouse us to the fact that every single second of conscious life is a miracle past reckoning, a marvel past all computation."
>
> [Cowley, pp. 57-78]

Albert Schweitzer puts it another way:

> When we are familiar with death, we accept each week, each day, as a gift. Only if we are able thus to accept life—bit by bit—does it become precious.
>
> [Schweitzer, quoted by Bortz, p. 241]

Older people may not fear death, but most do worry about the process of dying. Many of the older people I visit have expressed a great fear of the possible pain and indignity that may be a part of their dying. They often express their wish for a quick death, such as Oliver Wendell Holmes described.

All of a sudden and nothing first,
Just as bubbles do when they burst.

[Quoted by Bortz, p. 257]

Scott-Maxwell expresses fear of the indignities of extreme old age with illness, as well as the pain of dying.

We wonder how much older we have to become, and what degree of decay we may have to endure. We keep whispering to ourselves, "Is this age yet? How far must I go?" For age can be dreaded more than death. "How many years of vacuity? To what degree of deterioration must I advance?"

[Scott-Maxwell, p. 138]

In this situation, death is perhaps welcome.

Some want death now, as release from old age, some say they will accept death willingly, but in a few years. I feel the solemnity of death, and the possibility of some form of continuity. Death feels a friend because it will release us from the deterioration of which we cannot see the end. It is waiting for death that wears us down, and the distaste for what we may become.

These thoughts are with us always, and in our hearts we know ignominy as well as dignity. We are people to whom something important is about to happen.

[Scott-Maxwell, p. 138]

Unfortunately, the dying process has been increasingly extended as the medical profession learns more and more ways to delay what it often considers its ultimate enemy, death. About new technology that enables doctors to prolong the dying process, Dr. Bortz writes,

Montaigne wrote, "Death is the moment when dying ends." It is our job to shorten the interval between the start of dying and death. I hope that all of my patients' dyings are appropriately brief. . . . To be healthy until the end. That is our highest ideal.

[Bortz, p. 246]

Probably because of the recent ability to extend life and with it the dying process, much attention is currently being given to relief of pain, particularly for the dying. In an article in the January-February 1995 issue of *Modern Maturity*, Mary Batten writes:

It's now possible to control most human pain. Rarely should anyone have to accept acute or chronic pain, including cancer pain. A variety of old and new drugs and therapies can work to stop pain in its neurochemical tracks. "Relief is not awaiting a scientific breakthrough. We now have the methods we need to relieve pain," says Betty Ferrell, R.N., Ph.D., FAAN, associate research scientist at City of Hope National Medical Center in Duarte, California.

[Batten, "Take Charge of Your Pain," *Modern Maturity*, January-February 1995, p. 35]

Batten even provides a list of organizations working for pain relief and the names of several books on the subject, as well as a "pain patient's bill of rights" from a 1994 book called *Pain Relief* by Jane Cowles, Ph.D.

Mention should also be made here, as in any discussion of pain relief for the dying, of the hospice program, which offers the services of many disciplines to those who are in the advanced stages of illness. A hospice team does not seek to postpone death, but helps people live their remaining life fully, prepare for death, and maintain personal control over their lives as long as possible. Pain relief and symptom control are important parts of their mission, as is counseling for family members. In the two instances in my personal experience where a hospice team was called in, those closest to the dying person reported that the help given was of inestimable value.

In a clinical but sympathetic book written for the layperson, surgeon Dr. Sherwin B. Nuland describes the death of his own patients from common causes. He does not paint very pretty pictures. Like Dr. Bortz, he believes that pain can and should be alleviated, and that life should not be prolonged beyond reason. Concerning dying with dignity, he does not offer the hope that we would wish, a quick death or a slow fading away surrounded by loved ones. He points out in the beginning of the first chapter:

> Every life is different from any that has gone before it, and so is every death. The uniqueness of each of us extends even to the way we die.
>
> [Nuland, p. 3]

What he says about dignity and hope is worth pondering.

> The greatest dignity to be found in death is the dignity of the life that preceded it. This is a form of hope we can all achieve, and it is the most abiding of all. Hope resides in the meaning of what our lives have been.
>
> [Nuland, p. 242]

The spiritual aspect of facing death, which Nuland here brings to mind, is discussed toward the end of the second chapter.

Another view of the different ways of dying is spoken by the character Magda in *The Good Husband* by contemporary novelist Gail Godwin. Dying of cancer, Magda is hallucinating about telling her college students a story about a dying woman. It is really her own story.

> "Yes, dying," said Magda, pleased. "Irrevocably, unquestionably dying. She was done for and they all knew it. She lay there rotting away, because that was her destined mode of expiration. Some of us will be snuffed out quickly and painlessly, with with no time to reconnoiter the mysterious route by which we have arrived at where we are. Others of us are charted for a slower, more agonizing, exit, but with the consolation prize of being allowed to take stock of our lives as we lie there and disintegrate."
>
> [Godwin, p. 299]

On Death and Dying by Elisabeth Kubler-Ross is the classic book on how people view their own approaching death. Using her own clinical research, she describes usual stages of reaction to news of fatal illness: denial and isolation, anger, bargaining, depression, and acceptance. She says that

> the majority of our patients die in the stage of acceptance, an existence without fear and despair.
>
> [Kubler-Ross, p. 120]

This informative and compassionate book also includes the very interesting observation that

> patients die easier if they are allowed and helped to detach themselves slowly from all the meaningful relationships in their life.
>
> [Kubler-Ross, p. 118]

I found that observation echoed by May Sarton, writing several years before her death, when she was very ill. She said that she had been haunted by a passage written by Jung in the "wonderful book" *On Dreaming and Death.*

> It's about the fact that as one gets ready to die, one gradually gives up even affection, even love changes, because a great transformation is taking place.
>
> [Sarton, *Endgame*, p. 339]

After quoting the rather long passage, she says,

> This, when I'm going to sleep at night, is very much the feeling I have. It's strange, but personal relations do not mean what they did—there's no doubt. I am in some ways becoming very detached. It's possible that pain, to some extent, does this, but also that passage makes me understand something I've not understood all the years since my mother, the day before she died, said, "Take the flowers away." She had loved flowers so much. . . . Now I see that she was detaching herself almost by will.
>
> [Sarton, *Endgame*, p. 340]

My purpose is not to linger over the psychological or physical realities of dying and death but rather to acknowledge the fears experienced by older people and to suggest how we might view and attempt to lessen the fear of dying and death both for ourselves and for the "old old" with whom we converse.

A very serene and wise old woman summarized for me her attitude toward her present condition and imminent death in a gentle way I will never forget. Ella was a frail farm woman of eighty-five who had lost her sight and was dying of emphysema in a dirty, run-down cottage while cared for by her sloppy but devoted son. She had been taken to the hospital for heart and lung crises many times. She said quietly about it all, "While you are living, you live; and when you die, you die." One at a time, no point in worrying.

Eleanor Roosevelt had a similarly fatalistic but practical view. Regarding an afterlife, she wrote:

And I came to feel that it didn't really matter very much because whatever the future held you'd have to face it when you came to it, just as whatever life holds you have to face it in exactly the same way. . . .

And so I have tried to follow that out—and not to worry about the future or what was going to happen. I think I am pretty much of a fatalist. You have to accept whatever comes and the only important thing is that you meet it with courage and with the best that you have to give.

[Roosevelt, *Songs*, pp. 362-63]

Such a practical outlook appears from a slightly different angle in Vining's journal.

We each have some earthly task to do, and when it is done, we go home. . . .

The task, I think, is not an obvious one, not visible to the outward eye even of love. It must be some inner act of growth, some hidden contract to be met, some ripening to be accomplished. . . . Some ripen young; some take a long time to do it.

[Vining, pp. 125-26]

One hears echoes of Ecclesiastes' "a time to be born and a time to die." Some see death more as a passage than an end. Southern novelist Ellen Glasgow, in her autobiography, *The Woman Within*, writes of her near-death in terms echoed by others who have had a similar experience.

All I knew was that I had looked at death, which is the other side of life, and that death was "lovely and soothing. . . ." When I thought of dying, in those weary months of convalescence, it was not of dying as a cold negation, but as a warm and friendly welcome to the universe, to the Being beyond and above consciousness, or any vestige of self.

[Glasgow, *Songs*, p. 361]

Playwright Bertolt Brecht also sees death as a passage, but in a different way, as an end to this life's regrets and a chance to begin again.

What has happened has happened. The water
You once poured into the wine cannot be
Drained off again, but
Everything changes. You can make
A fresh start with your final breath.

[Brecht, *Songs*, p. 337]

My personal approach shares in all those described above. I summarize my beliefs in the image of each of us being held very gently in God's hand now and always. This expresses for me His love for us and His knowledge of what is best for each of us. I would use the words about God's love and wisdom that John Keats wrote about truth and beauty: "that is all / Ye know on earth, and all ye need to know."

Three Daily Challenges

By far, the three most common problems that I have encountered in visiting the "old old" are loneliness, boredom, and depression. Writers about the elderly often distinguish the "old old" from the "young old," and some even insert a middle period between the two. In general, the "young old" include those of us who are at least sixty years of age and still fully active. The age line between the two groups is usually drawn at about eighty to eighty-five years. The extent of mobility and mental acuity may move the line in either direction by a few years.

However, anyone over seventy who lives alone and is unable to walk well enough to leave home knows the problems of the "old old." Add blindness to the mixture—and some sight loss is not unusual—and the difficulties are multiplied. A degree of hearing loss, certainly more common than sight loss, makes communication difficult but does not cause as much dependence.

Although loneliness, boredom, and depression are the almost daily challenges facing the "old old," they loom only slightly off the scene for many of the "young old." They are closely interrelated and often occur in combination, but I shall discuss them separately here. Also briefly, because their prevalence hardly needs demonstration. The next chapter suggests ways to cope with them that have proven effective.

Loneliness

All the elders I visit at their homes, without exception, complain of loneliness as a major problem. They include those who live a stone's throw from their grown children and even some with a still-living mate in residence. From reading and personal experience, I know that loneliness is not limited to those seeking help through county programs. People of all ages experience loneliness at one time or another, but when one is old, circumstances causing loneliness are less likely to change for the better. The usually irreversible losses of old age, including mate, employment, driver's license, and mobility, tend to increase the amount of time an older person must spend alone.

The loneliness of the elderly has been described movingly by many authors. Here I shall give only two descriptions, one from a novel and the other from the famous memoirs of Scott-Maxwell.

In *The Summer House*, a novel by Alice Thomas Ellis, the author describes how loneliness can creep up on the old. Monica is speaking to herself, expressing amazement that she, an English middleclass woman, is lonely enough to socialize with a charwoman:

> I lay against the pillows thinking how undignified the neighbours would consider my conduct and my conversation with the charwoman, and how much I valued her. Without her, I reflected, I would be insupportably lonely. I had always heard that old age was a time of loneliness and it had never perturbed me, since I had imagined that what was meant was a physical separation from one's fellows. Old people who lived alone, cut off by distance, or senility, or simple crabbedness, were lonely—not me. I had kept myself to myself from choice and I had never understood until now that loneliness was not imposed from outside but had bred and spread in me until I had become its host, and little else. I had not realized until now that I was lonely.
>
> [Ellis, p. 224]

I have noticed similar friendships developing between lonely older women and those formerly considered simply "the help." Loneliness is powerful enough to dispel what may have been strong class distinctions in earlier years.

Scott-Maxwell describes the way I think many lonely elders feel:

> We live in a limbo of our own. Our world narrows, its steady narrowing is a constant pain. Friends die, others move away, some become too frail to receive us, and I become too frail to travel to them. Talk exhausts us, the expense of the telephone reduces us to a breathless rush of words, so that letters are our chief channel of friendship. Letters can be scarce so we tend to live in a world of our own making, citizens of Age, but otherwise stateless.
>
> [Scott-Maxwell, p. 137]

Boredom

Many of the lonely are also bored. Their lives too often consist merely of getting through the necessary steps of a day, sometimes laboriously. For the very old, just getting up and dressed, putting together simple meals, taking the re-

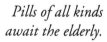

Pills of all kinds await the elderly.

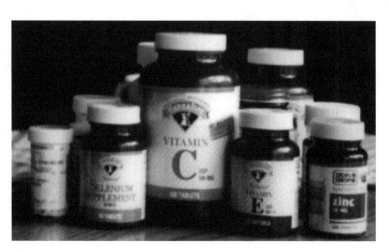

quired medicines, and preparing for bed are time-consuming tasks. And boring ones. For many, lack of stimulation makes their discomfort or pain more central. Therefore visits or telephone calls to the doctor become more important, absorbing, and frequent. Their lives become squeezed into a very small circle.

Bored people often think the solution for boredom is the same as for loneliness, that is, more people in their lives. They feel that their children, neighbors, and friends are neglecting them, and that is the reason they are bored. In most cases it has seemed to me that their children, if not their friends, were being as attentive as they could be without radically disrupting their own lives. I have so far visited only one older person who thought that her children were "doing enough" for her, and I wasn't sure that I agreed.

Boredom may apparently be experienced to some extent by the "old old"—at least those living alone and housebound—regardless of their talents, education, and accomplishment in prior years. An example is Scott-Maxwell, who had been a very active writer of short stories, plays, and books, as well as an activist for women's suffrage and a practicing analytical psychologist in her later years. Writing in 1968 at the age of eighty-five, she described vividly her situation:

> Another day to be filled, to be lived silently, watching the sky and the lights on the wall. No one will come probably. I have no duties except to myself. That is not true. I have a duty to all who care for me—not to be a problem, not to be a burden. I must carry my age lightly for all our sakes, and thank God I still can. Oh that I may to the end. Each day then, must be filled with my first duty, I must be "all right". But is this assurance not the gift we all give to each other daily, hourly?
>
> [Scott-Maxwell, p. 31]

Another description is found in *The Summer House*, when the aging Monica expresses very well the boredom that I have seen in the faces of many elders.

> How boring it was to live in the present, I thought; how banal the minutiae of everyday existence.
>
> [Ellis, p. 150]

Later, she complains more graphically.

> Yet another morning had come round. Life was like some debilitating, hypnotic game composed of endless repetition: some cosmic fruit-machine—mindless, mechanical, like the monsters in the pub by the river. The mere speeding succession of days was enough to unhinge the reason.
>
> [Ellis, p. 233]

Depression

Loneliness and boredom together usually lead to depression. I mean here not what is termed "clinical depression," which can often be alleviated by medication, but the ordinary, everyday "down" feeling that all of us have experienced to some degree. An important difference is that the very old often have few ways to escape loneliness and boredom completely, because losses that caused those problems cannot be reversed. "If I had not lost my husband/job/car/mobility, I would be fine."

Scott-Maxwell once more provides a vivid description of how the very frail or elderly often feel.

> Again a day that is so empty that I cry inside, a heavy weeping that will not stop. . . . The grey sky seems very grey, but I finally soothe myself by small duties, putting away freshly ironed linen, watering plants. Order, cleanliness, seemliness make a structure that is half support, half ritual, and if it does not create it maintains decency. I make my possessions appear at their best as they are my only companions. Some days it is the only improvement I can bring about.
>
> [Scott-Maxwell, pp. 129-30]

Depression, however, lies deeper than loneliness and boredom combined. It seems to be related to how we feel about ourselves—our past, present, and future. When we lack companions and activities to occupy our minds, when we face the blackness of empty days, one after the other, we have little escape from introspective thoughts of who we have or have not become, what we have or have not done with our lives, and what we can or cannot do with the possibly few days, months, or years left to us. Wayne Booth, in interesting text linking selections and quotations about aging, writes,

> Almost eveyone I know who is over sixty confesses, when I get up my courage and ask about regrets, to a deep sense of unfulfilled promise. Oh, the things I could have done, if only. . . . If only I had been brought up right, if only my parents had sent me to better schools, if only I hadn't been so lazy, if only I hadn't worked so generously on other people's problems, if only I had been from another ethnic background.
>
> [Booth, p. 68]

Stanley Jacobson, writing in *The Atlantic Monthly* at the age of seventy, sees depression in later years as the age-appropriate struggle to face one's own mortality, as

> the consequence of being stuck in the struggle—silently, secretly, hopelessly—because our culture all but forbids serious discussion of death as the inevitable end of life. . . . Oldness itself is reason to be sad if you dwell on it, and it is in any event a matter of life and death to contend with.
>
> [Jacobson, *The Atlantic Monthly*, April 1995, p. 46]

In discussing a report on life stages, he points out that

> old age is very different from all the others by virtue of being the last: it is the only stage that cannot be outlived, and it is the final opportunity to give definition to one's life, the last chance to do and be what one values.
>
> [Jacobson, p. 48]

Jacobson believes

Health professionals want to reduce the struggle of the old to an illness. They label it "depression," search for biological explanations of the "disease," and call the psychological, spiritual, and social aspects of the conflict mere "risk factors." Unfortunately, by colluding in the denial that the fact of our mortality is significant to our mental health in late life, they contribute more to the prevalence of depression than to its cure. Failure to credit the resilience and resourcefulness that successful aging requires (and that most people find within them) is a more significant public-health problem than late-life depression.

[Jacobson, p. 48]

He writes further about how normal it is for those who enjoy living to face their imminent mortality, pointing out that

we cannot both love life and be indifferent to dying. . . . And our consciousness of the saddening vicissitudes of late life does not presage a fall into a medically significant depression.

[Jacobson, p. 51]

I find Jacobson's removal of non-clinical depression from the category of illness very liberating. Depression remains unpleasant and something to combat, but it becomes a natural part of the human development that we call aging.

Six Possible Joys

While none of the elderly authors cited pretends that aging is without pain, many seem eager to tell us that out in their world something wonderful lies waiting to be discovered.

> Whatever poet, orator, or sage may say of it,
>   old age is still old age.
> It is the waning, not the crescent moon;
> The dusk of evening, not the blaze of noon.
> For age is opportunity no less
> Than youth itself, though in another dress.
> And as the evening twilight fades away
> The sky is filled with stars, invisible by day.
> [Longfellow, "Morituri Salutamus," Stanza 24]

"Stars, invisible by day." In youth and middle age, we observe in older people primarily the failing of body and sometimes mind, but we are usually unable to perceive rewards, because they are spiritual and thus less open to us.

However, at dusk—in early old age—the stars become discernible if we look up into the sky, knowing that they are there. The authors I will be quoting are assuring us that the stars of old age are indeed there, that they are at least as real as its pain. We who are the "young old" are able to understand because we may perhaps have had intimations ourselves.

Many of the authors cited view old age as a time of both opportunity and challenge—opportunity to discover and enjoy new experiences that come with old age and challenge to face the difficulties and to devise methods of overcoming them. They are all both realistic as well as inspiring. They are among the successful, articulate, and creative old, but they are not Pollyannas. They differ from most of the elderly I have known as a companion or counselor by their education, perhaps their imagination, and certainly their ability to communicate.

We can learn from them the many possibilities for enjoying old age in the hope that we may learn to see the "stars," and even perhaps help others to do so. Life seems to offer us a new dimension as we age.

Being Oneself

One of the earliest rewards is the pleasure and relief of being able to "be oneself." Listen to these authors rhapsodize.

First, May Sarton.

> I have been thinking about old age and how much I enjoy the freedom of it. By that I mean the freedom to be absurd, the freedom to forget things because everyone expects you to forget, the freedom to be eccentric, if that is what you feel like, or, on the other hand, the freedom to be quite rigid and to say, "But this is the way I do things."
>
> [Sarton, *Encore*, p. 41]

Eda LeShan says the experience is universal.

> Almost everyone I talked to about getting older commented on the "pleasure of speaking my mind."
>
> [LeShan, *50 Again,* p. 59]

M. F. K. Fisher obviously agrees, explaining her ability to be herself in terms of feeling accepted.

> I notice that as I get rid of the protective covering of the middle years, I am more openly amused and incautious and less careful socially, and all this makes for increasingly pleasant contacts with the world. (It also compensates for some of the plain annoyances of decrepitude, the gradual slowing down of physical things like muscles, eyes, bowels. In other words, old age is more bearable if it can be helped by an early acceptance of being loved and of loving.)
>
> [Fisher, "Afterword" in *Sister Age*, p. 235]

Betty Friedan, champion first of women and then of the aging, gives a very down-to-earth and personal description.

The hallmark of people who continue growing and developing is that they become more and more authentically themselves. You become more whole, you put it all together—the mistakes and triumphs, the pain and sadness and joy—and you stop stewing over what your mother or father didn't do when you were 6, or over your big nose or thick ankles. You become *comfortable with* yourself, the way you look. You don't care so much what other people think. You become a truth-teller.

[Friedan, *Parade Magazine*, March 20, 1994, pp. 5-6]

Florida Scott-Maxwell admits that this new freedom has its bad as well as good side.

One's appearance, a lifetime of effort put into improving that, most of it ill judged. Only neatness is vital now, and one can finally live like a humble but watchful ghost. You need not plan holidays because you can't take them. You are past all action, all decision. In very truth the old are almost free, and if it is another way of saying that our lives are empty, well—there are days when emptiness is spacious, and non-existence elevating.

[Scott-Maxwell, p. 119]

Elsewhere, she gives this delightful and amusing picture of herself.

My kitchen linoleum is so black and shiny that I waltz while I wait for the kettle to boil. This pleasure is for the old who live alone. The others must vanish into their expected role.

[Scott-Maxwell, p. 28]

Coming into our own involves not only speaking our minds and being more relaxed in relationships, but also the closely related acceptance of ourselves that makes us more integrated, independent, and effective. Elizabeth Coatsworth, a writer of children's books, writes at eighty-three.

During much of my life I was anxious to be what someone else wanted me to be. Now I have given up that struggle. I am what I am.

[Coatsworth, *Songs*, p. 29]

Anne Morrow Lindbergh phrases the same basic idea a bit differently in a 1983 speech.

One learns to walk alone, and that is one of the opportunities in age, a last chance to learn to be truly independent and free to choose one's life and interests and friends, enjoying them but not leaning on anyone. A state we dreamed of in adolescence but never quite found.

[Lindbergh, *Songs*, p. 267]

May Sarton ofttimes in her journals almost revels in the freedom of age, even before becoming one of the "old old."

My 65th year, just past has been the happiest and most fruitful so far. I do not see diminution except in sustained energy, but the lack of energy is more than made up for by my knowing better how to handle myself. . . . The best things about old age are so outside our ethos that we cannot, some of us, even imagine a state of growth that might have to do with contemplation, pure joy, and above all the elimination of the nonessential . . .

[Sarton, *The New York Times*, January 30, 1978, quoted by LeShan, *50 Again,* pp. 12-13]

Five years later, Sarton relates an amusing experience during one of her poetry readings.

In the course of it I said, "This is the best time of my life. I love being old." At that point a voice from the audience asked loudly, "Why is it good to be old?" I answered spontaneously and a little on the defensive, for I sensed incredulity in the questioner, "Because I am more myself than I have ever been. There is less conflict. I am happier, more balanced, and" (I heard myself say rather aggressively) "more powerful." . . . It might have been more accurate to say "I am better able to use my powers." I am surer of what my life is all about, have less self-doubt to conquer.

[Sarton, *At Seventy*, p. 10]

Think of all the joys expressed above. If you are not quite old enough to have experienced them yet, try to imagine them. Enjoying the freedom to do, say, and simply be what you wish. Feeling that you are accepted both by yourself and by others for what you are. Becoming more whole, growing into the person you sense you were born to be. Coming into self-assured possession of your latent abilities and the power that comes with it. All rather heady stuff. But is it available to us all as we age?

I can speak only from my own experience. In my mid-sixties, I at least know what these authors are talking about, and I suspect that most readers of my age will also. About fifteen years ago, I remember being very surprised when a friend, ten years my senior, began to display an attitude that I described to myself as a "what-the-hell" approach to life. She became less rigid about what her family did, she laughed more, and she started to pay less attention to her hair style and make-up. My surprise was followed by rather puzzled enjoyment. She was much better company. At that point, I didn't realize that I was about to grow into the same relaxed view of myself.

I first noticed this pleasant development after my remarriage. Perhaps it would have begun earlier if I had not been trying to find a mate and thus concerned with how I would appear to the opposite sex. Who knows. At any rate, it began with a devil-may-care attitude toward my appearance. I remained neat and clean, of course, and continued to use lipstick. But that was it. Working around the horses outside, I no longer set my hair every morning, only to have it go straight after an hour in the heat. I pulled it back into a bun and figured a smile would have to make up for the hair style. And although I didn't gain weight, I no longer chose clothing to show off the good points in my figure.

I also stopped explaining myself. New to the area, I might in earlier years have made sure that my new acquaintances learned about my career in Washington, D.C., my expertise with horses and dogs, the fine children I had raised, and whatever else distinguished me from the multitude. It didn't seem worth the effort. I knew who I was, what I had done, and also what I hadn't done that I might have done. I really had no urge to share the knowledge. I felt confident that eventually I would make friends just on the basis of the present me and the future me.

Nor did I join every local organization in an effort to become a part of the community. I applaud people who do this well and fruitfully and am thankful there are enough to go around without me. That is not, as they say, "my thing." I am a one-on-one person who has never learned to fit happily into the group scene. I am now ready to recognize and accept that I am simply made that way, like it or not.

Instead of working and playing in a group, I thoroughly enjoy sitting alone at my computer putting ideas into order and finding the most effective words to express them. I am passionate about horses, like to ride with one companion, and feel like a queen when astride a horse. Exploring trails and mapping them fascinates me, and fortunately my husband enjoys clearing them with me. I also find dogs and cats delightful companions, well worth the effort they require and the grief I always experience at their death. And of course I find my elderly friends, one at a time, a wonderful source of companionship and strength. I may have a passing regret that I am not somebody else and every so often I may give it another brief try, but the regret is indeed passing. This is what I mean by the freedom of aging. It feels very, very good.

Some few lucky people are able to happily be themselves in youth or middle age, and some unlucky ones live their entire life feeling subservient to the opinion of others. However, it seems to me that this ability to be oneself is widely experienced and is the earliest gift to the aging.

Remembering and Musing

Although I have never had a good memory, I must admit that it has definitely become worse over the past five years. I now come up to a word—a very familiar word—and discover it has slipped away. I run after it, and it keeps moving, just out of reach, something like a horse that does not want to be haltered. However, a horse will almost always allow a persistent owner to catch him eventually, whereas not persistence but abandonment of the chase has been for me the only effective solution for catching a really recalcitrant word. Add to this frustration the increasingly frequent nuisance of forgetting why I came upstairs, where I put the key, or what I did even just yesterday. Such experiences are common to most of us after the age of sixty, and usually we laugh them off, knowing that they are not only inevitable but shared by others our age.

Eva LeShan makes the distinction we need as she comments helpfully on this loss of memory.

> We need at this time in our lives to begin to distinguish between memory and remembrance. Memory is all the facts, all the data of our daily lives from beginning to end. . . .
> The answer is that unless there is a great deal more wrong with us than just forgetfulness, we are simply becoming more selective in what we remember.
>
> [LeShan, *50 Again*, pp. 75-76]

The distinction between memory and remembrance is not only a comforting thought to those of us who forget little things, but it also seems to be true. And the selectivity, as I am sure we have all noticed in elderly people, ofttimes leads to remembering their youth more vividly than their yesterdays.

"Remembrance" leads to the distracted musing of the "old old." I have often been conversing with someone in her eighties when I become aware that she is not really with me. Something we have said has led her off by association into some memory and she seems quite unaware of me for a moment. I suspect this is what is occurring in the minds of old people one sees sitting quietly and contentedly by themselves in the sunshine of their front yards. The musing state has been described in many stories and is perhaps not totally different from the drifting and remembering that we "young old" may do in the periods of waking from or drifting into sleep.

Polly Francis writes,

> Old age is not all pain and limitations. It holds its own joys and satisfactions. The time has come when musing replaces activities—when the sleepless hours are filled from the harvest of a well-stored mind.
>
> [Francis, *Songs*, p. 33]

Malcolm Cowley echos the same appreciation of memories:

> What passes through the minds of many is a stream of persons, images, phrases, and familiar tunes. For some that stream has continued since childhood, but now it is deeper; it is their present and their past combined. At times they conduct silent dialogues with a vanished friend, and these are less tiring—often more rewarding—than spoken conversations.
>
> [Cowley, pp. 13-14]

In Sarton's *Kinds of Love*, Christina remarks about her aged husband,

He says he is wide awake when he is dozing—he just seems not to be there. But he is very much somewhere else.

[Sarton, *Kinds of Love*, p. 257]

Musing can come in the middle of a conversation, producing the long, rambling monologues that sometimes occur with old people. Monica, in *The Summer House*, notices this about herself and remarks on the complexity of memories:

How difficult it is to keep to the point when you grow old. Not only because the brain cells are failing but because there is so much to explain. So much unharnessed, uncategorized experience leads up to each new episode—no matter how trivial. Each new happening is not new, but an echo, a reminder, or a repetition of something that has happened before—and quite possibly before that, and before that again.

[Ellis, p. 140]

In *The Memory of Old Jack*, Wendell Berry writes vividly of the musings of an elderly black farmer, comparing himself to an old dog.

But the present is small and the future perhaps still smaller. And what his mind is apt to do is leap out of that confinement, like an old dog, still strong, that has been penned up and then let loose in the one countryside that it knows and that it knew for a long time. But it is like an old dog possessed by an old man's intelligent ghost that remembers all it has seen and done and all the places it has known, and that goes back to haunt and lurk in those places. Some days he can keep it very well in hand, just wandering and rummaging around in what he remembers. He is amazed at what he comes upon that he thought he had forgot.

[Berry, p. 31]

Enjoying Small Things

Elderly authors suggest that the old man we have seen sitting alone in his front yard, if not musing about his life, may be relishing the blue of the sky or the shape of a leaf in a way that he never did in his younger days.

Cowley describes how the old man feels. He speaks of

simply sitting still, like a snake on a sun-warmed stone, with a delicious feeling of indolence that was seldom attained in earlier years. A leaf flutters down; a cloud moves by inches across the horizon. At such moments the older person, completely relaxed, has become a part of nature—a living part, with blood coursing through his veins. The future does not exist for him.

[Cowley, p. 12]

Musing often has a spiritual element. Sarton describes the "bliss" of enjoying the small things in her novel, *Kinds of Love*.

Jane sighed and folded her hands together as if she clasped her intimate self between them. . . . She sighed and rocked, and felt the tensions slowly flow out. After a while she picked a sweet geranium leaf off the pot on the window sill beside her and rubbed it before inhaling its pungence. How little people knew about very old age! It would be quite absurd to mention to anyone—least of all to Hannah—that this scent of rose geranium filled her with what might be called bliss. As far as the senses go, she was thinking, we still live in large part in and through them. Very small things—apparently small, such as a mushroom, or a cup of tea, or a half-remembered line of poetry that suddenly came into focus and brought back the whole poem, or the delicious luxury of clean sheets—these little things now made the difference between hell and heaven. Sometimes Hannah's rough hand smoothing her pillow, or one of her awkward gestures of affection, became angelic.

[Sarton, *Kinds of Love*, pp. 133-34]

In the same novel, the aging Christina writes in her diary about seeing a pair of bluebirds, adding that

perhaps one of the gifts of old age is that nothing stands between us and what we see. The bluebirds gave me a lift like love itself.

[Sarton, *Kinds of Love*, p. 401]

At the age of seventy, Carter Catlett Williams was explicit about finding spiritual nurture and wisdom in his new appreciation of "plain things":

As I advance inexorably in the ranks of the older generation, plain things bring surprising gifts of the spirit. In these moments *things* signify, *routines* transform and are transforming, *relationships* weave patterns of surpassing richness. Plain things become the stuff of wonder, the source of new understanding, the assurance of things unseen, the sacraments of daily living.

[Williams, *Oxford*, p. 132, italics in original]

Bernard Berenson in his eighties believes that

awareness is the compensation that age gives us in exchange for mere action. . . .
    While everything else physical and mental seems to diminish, the appreciation of beauty is on the increase.

[Berenson, *Songs*, pp. 121-22]

Polly Francis agrees that

old age sharpens our awareness.

[Francis, *Songs*, p. 32]

Poet Eve Merriam believes that awareness in old age is directed toward little, everyday things:

I think that a love for the ordinary is what is most important as one ages, not for the extraordinary. There are always trips to Bali or Yokohama or Paris, but to get joy out of the daily-ness—that's what struck me when I hit my sixties. I thought, Good heavens, I'm getting so much pleasure out of my breakfast. I didn't know grapefruit juice could taste so good. This is really amazing. It's as though some kind of slight film over the world has been stripped away and there is now a clarity that one didn't have before.

[Merriam, *Ageless*, p. 197]

A single red tulip reveals special beauty to the eye and heart.

Scott-Maxwell gives the same idea a more physical slant.

> The woman who has a gift for old age is the woman who delights in comfort. If warmth is known as the blessing it is, if your bed, your bath, your best-liked food and drink are regarded as fresh delights, then you know how to thrive when old. If you get the things you like on the simplest possible terms, serve yourself lightly, efficiently and calmly, all is almost well.
>
> [Scott-Maxwell, p. 88]

Fisher credits this special appreciation of small things to an increased intensity.

> Old age brings a special kind of sensitivity, a special kind of intensity to things. . . .
> I can concentrate more and I enjoy things in a way that I never did before. As an older person, I feel, for instance, the color of that strange flower at the end of the table more intensely than when I was younger, although I was very aware of it when I was younger.
>
> [Fisher, *Sister Age*, p. 93]

The intensity she notes is the fourth reward, discussed below.

Living Intensely

I am describing the rewards of becoming old in the order in which it seems to me they tend to appear chronologically. This same order, perhaps by coincidence, seems also to apply to their likelihood. Most of us over sixty enjoy saying what we think and behaving as we wish, not worrying over much about how we appear to others. This is certainly true of most of the "old old" I know. The second reward, remembering and musing, appears to increase as activity decreases, so that we "young old" do some of it when we have the time, while those older people we visit, being less active, are doing more remembering and musing. As for the third reward, it is hard to tell if the "old old" people I visit take greater pleasure in little things than they used to. None ever has said so.

Of course many people in nursing homes, lonely and deprived by their frailty of all activity, anticipate food and small gifts more than they would have earlier, but this may simply be because there is nothing else. In other words, I am wondering if increased pleasure in small things, so enthusiastically described by the authors above, is less available to everyone than the other rewards. Perhaps it is reserved for those with more than average sensitivity, creativity, or imagination.

Certainly the fourth reward—intensity of living—is not seen daily among the old. Scott-Maxwell believes it arrives late, for those in their eighties:

> Age puzzles me. I thought it was a quiet time. My seventies were interesting, and fairly serene, but my eighties are passionate. I grow more intense as I age. To my own surprise I burst out with hot conviction. Only a few years ago I enjoyed my tranquillity; now I am so disturbed by the outer world and by human quality in general that I want to put things right, as though I still owed a debt to life. I must calm down. I am far too frail to indulge in moral fervour.
>
> [Scott-Maxwell, pp. 13-14]

While celebrating intensity, she does not forget the pain of old age.

> We who are old know that age is more than a disability. It is an intense and varied experience, almost beyond capacity at times, but something to be carried high. If it is a long defeat it is also a victory, meaningful for the initiates of time, if not for those who have come less far.
>
> [Scott-Maxwell, p. 5]

Intensity is very much a bittersweet experience, at times almost an epiphany, hard for her to describe.

> Another secret we carry is that though drab outside—wreckage to the eye, mirrors a mortification—inside we flame with a wild life that is almost incommunicable. . . .
>
> It is a place of fierce energy. Perhaps passion would be a better word than energy, for the sad fact is this vivid life cannot be used. If I try to transpose it into action I am soon spent. . . . It is just life, the natural intensity of life, and when old we have it for our reward and undoing. It can—at moments—feel as though we had it for our glory. Some of it must go beyond good and bad, for at times—though this comes rarely, unexpectedly—it is a swelling clarity as though all was resolved. It has no content, it seems to expand us, it does not derive from the body, and then it is gone. It may be a degree of consciousness which lies outside activity, and which when young we are too busy to experience.
>
> [Scott-Maxwell, pp. 32-33]

Maurice Goudeket writes of this experience in a more specific way.

> I get up before anyone else in my household, not because sleep has deserted me in my advancing years, but because an intense eagerness to live draws me from my bed. In the same way I drop off every night with a kind of secret satisfaction as I think of the day to

come, even if it is likely to be a dark one; for tomorrow is the future and tomorrow contains the whole of that which is possible.

[Goudeket, p. 6]

May Sarton's journals also give clear evidence of intensity in the later years.

Gaining Perspective

The fifth and sixth rewards are in the spiritual realm. They involve a standing back from life, an assessment of what is of value. Robert Butler, an American geriatrician and writer, believes that an attempt to gain perspective on one's life comes automatically with sufficient age.

I conceive of the life review as a naturally occurring, universal mental process characterized by the progressive return to consciousness of past experiences, and, particularly, the resurgence of unresolved conflicts; simultaneously, and normally, these revived experiences and conflicts can be surveyed and reintegrated.

[Butler, *Oxford*, p. 381]

He speculates that an increasing awareness of mortality sparks these reminiscences and reassessments.

Presumably, this process is prompted by the realization of approaching dissolution and death, and the inability to maintain one's sense of personal invulnerability. It is further shaped by contemporaneous experiences and its nature and outcome are affected by the life-long unfolding of character.

[Butler, *Oxford*, p. 381]

Actor and author Ossie Davis phrases the thought in simpler language and carries it one step further.

From experience, I would say that age is that point of elevation from which it is easier to see who you are, what it is you want to do, and from which you find yourself closer to the very center of the universe. . . . I think age gives you the possibility of thinking with less distortion—distortion that in the beginning was created by ego, by passion, by sex, by love, by ambition, by many things. And as you encounter the distortions and as you go through the periods in your life and correct them, they fall into a certain pattern and you realize that the thing that you thought was absolutely essential wasn't really essential at all, it was a part of something else.

[Davis, *Ageless*, pp. 64-65]

The gleaning of the nonessential from the essential that Davis notes gives the English writer Sybil Harton a sense of freedom.

With increasing age we become blessedly free from the urge to conserve, from the necessity to plan and to buy for the future, to keep this and that for possible reference. No longer is there any need to hang on to anything, but with glad largesse we can give away our treasures to younger generations and feed on the delight this gives to others.

[Harton, p. 125]

Although the elders I visit give few signs of some of the other possible joys that I have enumerated, many have shown delight in giving away things they are not using and also in planning who will receive which of their treasures when they "no longer need them," to use the popular phrase. One of my elderly friends, who lives in a tiny house and receives an equally tiny income, has written a friend's or relative's name on the back of each of the ten clocks in her living room, and often tells me of other items that she will leave to relatives, friends, and others providing services through the local home care agency. She also enjoys giving me and others some of the coupons she receives in the mail. Part of her pleasure comes from being able to give at least something back to the people who are giving their time and services to her with little or no monetary compensation.

Harton finds not only the pleasure of giving but a buoyancy in the act of no longer wanting one's physical possessions.

> To be absolutely free of things at any time confers a wonderful liberty. . . . The progressive withdrawal of our interest in possessions which are personal brings a spiritual lightness and nobility which act as wings in raising the soul to its true home.
>
> [Harton, p. 125]

LeShan confirms the tendency of age to lead to a new spirituality.

> I came to agree with my husband Larry's theory that as you get older there's an unconscious moving toward the spiritual, a desire to be part of the universe as a whole, and that it is a kind of preparation for death. It's about moving beyond a state of denial toward a deeper and deeper sense of appreciation of life itself.
>
> [LeShan, *Ageless*, p. 156]

Poet Stanley Kunitz writes of a very different but equally spiritual by-product of one's increasing perspective.

> I suppose my basic view of experience is that our life is tragic and yet it is full of comedy, and the very fact that you take yourself so seriously is one of its comic aspects. Measured against the whole cosmos none of us is important.
>
> [Kunitz, *Ageless*, p. 135]

His comments suggest a peaceful acceptance of the ironies of life and a cessation of struggle. A type of wisdom.

Becoming Wise

The sixth reward is completely spiritual and certainly not found in all the elderly. Yet it is the goal to be reached, in one form or another, depending upon each individual.

Sarton's Christina describes in her diary an acceptance reminiscent of that suggested by Kunitz, but blended with joy.

This is the year when we have learned to grow old, Cornelius and I. How I have dreaded it all my life—the giving up, the "not being able" to do this or that. But now that we are here, and truly settled in, it is like a whole new era, a new world, and I have moments of pure joy such as I never experienced before. It has to be set against pain, fatigue, exasperation of being caught in a dying body, but when I see the tears shining in Cornelius's eyes when he is moved, I feel as if every day the naked soul comes closer to the surface. He is so beautiful now.

[Sarton, *Kinds of Love*, pp. 462-63]

Maurice Goudeket, at the age of seventy-five, after expressing surprise at having lived so long, writes of a similar daily joy that has come to him in his later years.

For my own part, when the figure 75 happens to force itself upon my attention, my first reaction is astonishment. How can I possibly have got so far? Have I not made some mistake in my reckoning? They tell me I am so absentminded. What is to be done, where am I to go, and who is going to listen to my complaint? But the next moment I calm down: after all, it is really something of a feat to have lived seventy-five years, in spite of illnesses, germs, accidents, disasters, and wars. And now every fresh day finds me more filled with wonder and better qualified to draw the last drop of delight from it. For up until now I had never known time's inexpressible wealth; and my youth had never entirely yielded itself to happiness. Is it indeed this that they call growing old, this continual surge of memories that comes breaking in on my inner silence, this contained and sober joy, this lighthearted music that bears me up, this wider window on the world, this spreading kindly feeling and this gentleness?

[Goudeket, pp. 4-5]

Sarton echoes Goudeket as she writes that Christina's old flame asks her,

"What is young love compared to this—this incomparable truth of old age—that nothing dies, all is transformed?"

[Sarton, *Kinds of Love*, p. 452]

Experiences described above, although related to those of any age, are clearly reserved for old age. It is also clear that they are gifts that depend on who we are when we enter this last stage of development. A paragraph in Dr. Bortz's book provides hope that many of us who live long enough may gain wisdom.

My wonderful old patients are generally in communion with their own aging. They may lament physical losses, but on the whole they demonstrate a much greater sense of wholeness, of equanimity with life, than do my younger charges. Age has it many credits; and wisdom, gained from experience, is high among them. To change that which can be changed, rather than to batter at the unchangeable. The wisdom to know the difference. This resolve seems particularly evident in my older patients. Sickness always hurts, but it hurts less in the older years.

[Bortz, p. 43]

The same idea in very different clothing is expressed by the Skin Horse, as he explains to the Velveteen Rabbit what becoming "Real"—read "wise"—means.

> "Generally, by the time you are Real, most of your hair has been loved off, and your eyes drop out and you get loose in the joints and very shabby. But these things don't matter at all, because once you are Real you can't be ugly, except to people who don't understand."
>
> [Margery Williams, *The Velveteen Rabbit*, p. 17]

Robert Louis Stevenson phrases the idea of an appropriate development throughout life this way.

> The true wisdom is to be always seasonable, and to change with a good grace in changing circumstances. To love playthings well as a child, to lead an adventurous and honourable youth, and to settle, when the time arrives, into a green and smiling age, is to be a good artist in life and deserve well of yourself and your neighbour.
>
> [Stevenson, quoted by Booth, p. 252]

The aging process is compared to that of a sunflower's ripening, a natural and to-be-wished-for development.

> Aging? You never hear of anything in nature aging, or a sunflower saying, "Well, I'm growing old," and leaning over and vomiting. You know, it *ripens*, it drops its seed and the cycle goes on. So I'm ripening. For "Age" you can say "ripening."
>
> [Meridel Le Sueur, *Oxford*, p. 95]

Sarton describes a very old friend, Lotte Jacobi, in a way that must make everyone who reads the passage wish to have known her.

> She grew old in the way of a fairy godmother, more charming and irresistible with every year—until the very end, when for a few years she was not quite herself, though still a creature of joy and lightning response, a mischievous smile, a sense of herself as having much to give. . . . And the people who had come to her for years for wisdom and a taste of that rich life still came when the life had become a little askew, because, not quite all there, she was more there than most people ever are.
>
> [Sarton, *Endgame*, p. 25]

Another friend, Juliette Huxley, is pictured similarly as

> somebody ninety-five who forgets almost everything but then suddenly remembers everything and is still so full of charm and humor and love that to be with her is a sheer blessing and joy.
>
> [Sarton, *Encore*, p. 229]

LeShan tells of discovering May Sarton and her own gradual awareness of what old age can be.

> One of the greatest joys of my middle years was the discovery of the poet May Sarton. I just happened upon one of her books of fiction in a Cape Cod library, and within a week

I had read everything I could find written by her. Her conclusion of an article on the subject of aging was

> Old age is not an illness, it is a timeless ascent.
> As power diminishes, we grow toward more light.
> [*The New York Times Magazine*, January 30, 1978]

It has taken me about eight years and the writing of this book to begin to understand that philosophic and poetic synthesis of both acceptance and exultancy.

[LeShan, *50 Again*, p. 333]

Scott-Maxwell, on the other hand, rails against the narrowness of her life as she searches more for tranquility than joy. Her struggle for "quiet" runs throughout *The Measure of My Days*.

> When you reach this mute place you have no need to speak. It is no longer possible; and because you are cornered you are somehow saved. It is again the inner citadel, and unable to state it, incapable of in any way describing it, you only know that there in that one place is the relief of quiet.

[Scott-Maxwell, p. 45]

What peace she acquires is hard won against the intensity that she often feels.

> It takes increasing courage to be "I" as one's frailty increases. There is so little strength left that one wants shelter, one seeks the small and natural, but where to find it?
> A garden, a cat, a wood fire, the country, to walk in woods and fields, even to look at them, but these would take strength I have not got, or a man whom also I have not got. So, here in a flat, I must make the round of the day pleasant, getting up, going to bed, meals, letters with my breakfast tray: can I make it total to a quiet heart? I have to be a miracle of quiet to make the flame in my heart burn low, and on some good days I am a miracle of quiet. But I cannot conceive how age and tranquillity came to be synonymous.

[Scott-Maxwell, pp. 130-31]

She emphasizes the struggle, yet wonders if perhaps the peace is a natural gift of aging:

> Tranquility is not a grace waiting for us to take on as our right, but something we have to win with effort. It may not be our doing. It may be what facing age does to us.

[Scott-Maxwell, p. 144]

An arresting and interesting picture of a peaceful old man is drawn by William Wordsworth.

> The little hedgerow birds,
> That peck along the road, regard him not.
> He travels on, and in his face, his step,
> His gait, is one expression: every limb,
> His look and bending figure, all bespeak
> A man who does not move with pain, but moves
> With thought—He is insensibly subdued

To settled quiet: he is one by whom
All effort seems forgotten; one to whom
Long patience hath such mild composure given,
That patience now doth seem a thing of which
He hath no need. He is by nature led
To peace so perfect that the young behold
With envy, what the Old Man hardly feels.

[Wordsworth, "Animal Tranquility and Decay"]

A Natural Development

I think we all would like to realize the possible joys discussed above, but perhaps we either harbor some doubt that they really do exist—despite the witness of those describing them—or wonder if they are restricted to a talented and fortunate few. When I am listening to certain elderly women tell how empty their days are, how out of breath they become, how this and that hurts, how they have nothing to look forward to, and how no one really cares about them, the joys of aging indeed seem far away and even imaginary. Then I remember that Sarton and Scott-Maxwell—so eloquent on the rewarding experiences of aging — also had their very low times, often lonely, depressed, and fearful of complete dependence on others. Aging is an uphill climb, despite some great views near the top.

Having already tasted a few of the late-in-life joys myself and being able to imagine the rest, I believe that they are there for our taking if we proceed wisely. I am bolstered in this belief by how natural such a development seems as we age.

Sixty-some years is a long time to have lived. I have often tried to reassure younger friends by pointing out: "You will understand more about it and be able to handle it better when you are older." In face of their obvious disbelief that older people might know a little more than they do, I have asked this question: "Do you know more now, at age thirty-five, than you did at age twenty-five?" At their reluctant agreement, since by now they know where I am heading, I have made my point with: "So, if you keep on thinking throughout your life, don't you expect to learn something more each year?" Simply living a long time produces that irreplaceable commodity, experience.

My point is that, through trial and error, by our mid-sixties we ought to have learned a lot about what works in which situation. Experience should have taught us that attempts to please other people and thereby to get their approval often fail. And even if we acquire not only approval but even admiration, we rarely feel contented for very long. We learn that we might as well relax and be ourself, since there is little to be gained by trying to be what we guess someone else wants us to be. It may take us many years to discover this, but it is part of a natural progression if we live long enough, think about our life, and are not hindered by early injuries to our sense of self worth. Another impetus in the same direction comes from the physical deterioration that may begin to show itself somewhere in our sixties, if not earlier. We have a few aches and pains and may tire more easily, so that the effort to please others is simply not worth the little that we may—or may not—get out of it. The clincher is the feeling of joyful freedom that ensues when at last we end the years of trying for others' approval. I have written above of my own experience of that freedom.

As we relax into being ourselves, our center of spiritual balance may gradually change. It may move from "out there" with others toward "in here," in our own minds and souls. That movement is helped along by the reduction of social contacts that often occurs when we retire, can no longer drive, or lose a mate and friends to death. We have more time to be alone with ourselves, and while doing daily tasks we are apt to meditate, to think about our life, and perhaps instinctively to reach out to something both inside and beyond us. We may find ourselves praying without words.

However, even if surrounded by mate, children, and friends, we are likely to undergo slow, subtle change toward being our own person. Adult children, even married and living independently, seem to feel and behave differently in the presence of their parents. I remember struggling against my own regression when visiting my parents' home, even when with my husband and children. I knew that somehow I was not the same independent, self-assured person as I had become in my own home, away from their very strong influence. My parents did not live long enough into my adult life for me to succeed in completely conquering this tendency.

I have since wondered if my parents were completely themselves in my presence, because the person I am when alone is not exactly the person I am when with any of my children. Over the years I have moved very far toward being who I really am rather than being "mother." I still perceive a slight leaning off my center toward them, not to gain approval, but perhaps to provide a good example. My development has occurred very gradually, undoubtedly partly in response to their becoming more mature as they progressed through their thirties.

I am far from alone in my incomplete spiritual centering. As I mentioned earlier, every one of the elderly ladies with whom I have worked has acquired the ability to be pretty much herself. This does not mean that they all have a robust self-confidence—far from it. Nor do I think that they, any more than I, have attained a completely centered spiritual balance. I will give an example that should help clarify the distinction I am making between the very usual state of "being oneself" and the less frequently attained experience of "being centered in one-self."

Antonia, in her late seventies, lives alone in a large low-income apartment building for seniors. She needs hearing aids and a cane or a walker. She also suffers with a host of internal problems that apparently sap her energy. As long as she was physically able to do so, Antonia worked hard in many different blue-collar jobs. When I first met her, I immediately noticed her extreme eagerness to please and also a tendency to put herself down inappropriately. Although she feels sufficiently at ease to tell me all about her past and present life, she rarely turns her pale blue eyes directly toward me when she speaks. I decided that here was a person with absolutely no self-confidence.

With time, I learned that her manner belies strength of a certain kind. She has refused to have any contact with a daughter who has consistently been rude and inconsiderate toward her. She is hurt by her daughter, but she says, "I am not going to let that ruin my life. I don't need her. I can get along fine just by myself." She is justifiably proud of the prudence and restraint she exhibits in managing her meager income. Although she enjoys the company of other women and talk-ing with me about their motivations and relationships, she withholds her com-pany from people whom she considers gossips. "I will have none of that!" she declares. While I certainly do not think that all her attitudes and actions are wise, I do recognize that she has learned to "be herself." I read her as saying, "To heck with the others. I know who I am and I'm O.K."

I have not figured out the source of Antonia's self-deprecating manner. She loves to describe her "wonderful" childhood in a small farming community in southern Vermont. I do know that her marriages were a disaster, but she has never even implied any physical or psychological abuse. I have to assume that someone, sometime, made her feel worthless, and she has not recovered from that injury. Nevertheless, as she has grown older, she has begun to be very much herself. That she thoroughly enjoys this development is quite clear. And yet I feel that Antonia is always leaning out toward others in an attempt to somehow appease. While valuing herself as she is, she is not convinced that anyone else will find her acceptable. She wants and needs verification of her worth from others.

Although the very common joy of "being oneself" does not always reach its full bloom in a centering into oneself, it nevertheless is one step in the path toward spiritual development. It does not mean that we cease to adapt to other people and their needs. I am speaking of a movement of soul, not what actions we take in the world outside us. And for this movement to occur, some time completely alone is necessary.

Solitary meditation and prayer are tools people have used throughout the ages to become more attuned to the universe and themselves. What many have found — and I among them—is an influx of "something other," something immense, powerful, and personal, which most people identify with the all-powerful creator of the universe in terms defined by their particular cultural ancestors. For me, this is the God of the Hebraic-Christian tradition. The influx involves an experience of belonging, of being a part of whatever the universe is, of being accepted for what we are and will be, even of being treasured. Because solitude fosters spiritual development, the losses that leave many elderly people alone for hours may provide an excellent seeding ground for such an experience.

Another seed that often grows in such a soil is the second joy I discussed, a heightening and deepening of pleasure in small things. We have more time to marvel at the tiny flower at our feet, look it up in a book, and identify it as perhaps a maiden pink. We may have noticed it when we were younger, but then we had to chase across the meadow after one of our children or hurry home to make dinner in time to attend an evening meeting. Or if we saw a beautiful sunset, when we were younger we were more apt to run for the camera and record the sight for posterity. Now we have the sense not to record for the future but to savor in the present, not to think about showing the photograph of a sunset to our friends but to drink it in ourselves, perhaps wondering how many more such gorgeous views we will come upon in our lifetime.

There is also more opportunity and inclination for thinking about the past — and of course more past to think about than when we were younger. There is less time pressure. Even if we are busy all day, we can let our mind wander over earlier experiences as we go to sleep at night and slowly awaken in the morning. We need not be in such a hurry, day or night. Five or even fifteen minutes more or less will not make us miss a train and be late for work. A bit less sleep will make no difference to our efficiency on the job.

Remembrance for me is entirely spontaneous. Something inside my head brings up what it wishes, and I sort of look at it for awhile. I wonder why I did this or that, and would it have been better had I done something else. Sometimes I reword past conversations. Other times I just visualize different people I have known, or see in my mind my children at different ages, tasting the nostaligic pleasure of my passionate love for them as little ones. How beautiful they were, how wonderful it was to pick them up as they ran toward me. All sorts of things, good and bad, sometimes distressing, usually not. My periods of remembrance are usually in a half-waking state. The quotations given above to illustrate remembrance sound very real to me.

The accumulation of experience, the centering of spiritual balance inside ourselves, and the increase in time for spiritual pursuits all lead us to develop in still other ways. One more very important ingredient is the awareness that our life is coming to an end, day by day. We become like a child with a steadily decreasing amount of ice cream who decides to eat slowly, taste every little nuance of the flavor, and so make the pleasure last longer. We realize that every moment is precious, so we tend to focus on it and squeeze every bit of living out of it. Hence the intensity described by so many aging authors.

The awareness of death lurking down the path, behind some bush or tree perhaps, has already strongly influenced my own life. I mentioned above that my second husband and I married as recently as 1991. I was sixty-one years old, and he had just slipped over into being seventy. We consciously made the choice to "go for it," not to just go along living in the same place and doing the same things, but to make our later years memorable. We made a decision that some would think foolish. We moved many miles north to a rural community where, if we could no longer drive, we would be isolated. We also started to care for our own horses in a small pasture, meaning at least twice-a-day feeding and frequent manure removal even during long New England winters. Friends asked us, "What will happen when you are too old to drive? How will you care for your animals if one of you becomes sick? Wouldn't it be wiser to enter a retirement community where you will be assured of care in your old age?"

The point of the story is not that we chose a certain amount of risk, which we did, but that, having made the choice, we cannot but be aware that our present lifestyle will not last forever. We know that we will not always be able to hike together through the forests and bike along the country roads. The early morning clean-up routine and other horse-related tasks that we both enjoy will one day have to be delegated to someone we hope we will be able to afford to hire. We will not be able to drive off any evening we choose to attend a concert or play in a nearby city. The result, of course, is that we relish these activities all the more. Always in the back of our minds is the knowledge that in five, ten, maybe fewer years our idyllic life will have disappeared. We see friends younger than we having heart attacks and strokes. One is dying of cancer. And as even my forty-year old daughter recently began to realize for herself—much to my amusement at what to her was a discovery—the older you get, the faster time passes. So I taste many of my current pleasures with more intensity than I would have ten years ago when life seemed to stretch out far ahead.

Turning to the last two rewards, "gaining perspective" and "becoming wise," it may be helpful to use the idea of working on a picture puzzle as a simile for trying to understand our lives. Envision a puzzle of perhaps a thousand pieces. In

A picture puzzle nears completion. Anne Killay, librarian at the Moore-Leland Library in North Orange, Massachusetts, makes puzzles available to community members, who work on them separately and together.

our later years, we have more than half of the pieces in place, but we know that our time to finish the puzzle is limited. We are far enough along with it to have some idea of what the picture is going to be. In that situation, it is natural for us to speculate as to what the entire puzzle will look like, to be in a position to make a better guess as to where each piece is likely to fit.

Similarly, by our late sixties we have lived enough of our life to be able to get some perspective on it, to see what it means. While the final pieces are going into the puzzle, when we have reached a point where we think we see our lives as they have been, we may have years yet to live. At this time the benefits of earlier spiritual development should become especially important. We may not be thinking of death all the time, but the thought obviously cannot be far off. I see it surfacing every so often in the elderly I visit, sometimes only in very casual remarks, starting with, "When I am gone."

The time spent thinking about life, meditating, and praying may bring a familiar and comforting sense of being already a part of something larger, of belonging to the universe, even of being held spiritually safe in the hand of God. We may see ourselves as one small, beautiful note in a large, harmonious composition of which we are only a tiny, but essential, part. And be joyful that we are that one note. We may know ourselves secure enough to die easily, perhaps in physical pain but with spiritual ease.

I continually marvel at the way a human being is made. As the body begins to wear out with the passing of time, that very process produces the elements that may lead to spiritual growth that, in turn, may lead to acceptance of the body's death. Years of living produce experience, which along with a decrease in energy helps us to learn to be ourselves and often to center our spirits in ourselves. The decline in our physical abilities eventually leads to a decrease or cessation of work, which in turn produces more time for our increasingly spiritual self to muse about our past life and to appreciate small things. Then the approach of the death of the body completes the picture by making us value our time and so live more intensely. And as our physical life nears its completion, we are enabled to get an overall picture and discover its meaning. If all has gone well, wisdom and acceptance result.

But how often does all go well? Clearly, not always. Perhaps more to the point is the question: what can we do to make "all go well" for ourself? How can we age successfully, avoiding the fears, overcoming the challenges, and discovering the special joys that give an extra dimension to life?

Keys to Success

To know how to grow old is the master-work of wisdom, and one of the most difficult chapters in the great art of living.

[Henri Amiel, quoted by Bortz, p. 6]

Beginning Well

Acknowledging Old Age

Puzzlement has been the response of several people in their sixties and seventies whom I have told about my motives for writing this book. "Preparing for old age? I try not to think about it. Anyway, what is there to prepare for? It will just come someday, and meanwhile I will keep on doing what I am doing as long as I can." These same people have not been physically and mentally active, and I can see that they have at least the beginning signs of old age, whether they have chosen to recognize it or not.

I have met a similar response to my enthusiasm over the possible joys of old age. "Joys? What do you mean? My body will be wearing out. I had better enjoy as many pleasures now as I can." The change in words from "joys" to "pleasures" itself indicates a failure to understand what I am talking about.

Few of us really want to think about old age, perhaps because we are afraid to face the time when the body and perhaps the mind simply wear out. And often the closer we approach to old age, the more energy we spend avoiding the thought.

We have this ache and that pain, but they are only temporary. They will disappear shortly. And perhaps if we take another vitamin or herb we will live ten, twenty, thirty years longer. So why plan? It is so far off.

I am reminded of a very intelligent, kind woman whose "let's not think about it" attitude has surprised me. She has seen two parents grow old and die. One of the two could almost be said to have died of boredom. The other developed dementia. Her good friend is struggling with the vicissitudes of life in a nursing home. My friend shakes her head with pity and visits the nursing home, but she apparently does not entertain the notion that her own old age might not be a bowl of cherries. And perhaps she will have that bowl of cherries, translated as loving family nearby, plenty of books to read, an adequate income, and something to actively occupy her mind and hands. Some people are very lucky. I do wonder, however, if she will be able to savor as many of the special pleasures of old age as she might have if she were made aware that they exist. In fact, she may consciously block some of them, such as musing, because she associates them with aging. In a sense, the previous section on possible joys was written for her and those like her.

Some people in their sixties keep themselves too busy to give future years a thought. They have retired and they travel. When boredom or discontent of any kind is seen peeking around the corner, they quickly book another trip and the apparition disappears. That solves that. Until the travel palls, the money runs out, or the strain of frequent travel is just too much for their wearying bodies. Travel can both interest and delight, it has the reputation of "broadening the mind," and it provides something to talk about with one's peers. It does not, however, prepare one for perhaps many years of being unable to leave home. Pictures taken in exotic places lose their interest for others and even for oneself.

Grandchildren provide another way to be so busy that we cannot think of the years ahead. Like travel, this path is not all bad. In fact, it is in some ways good, because we are interacting with people more intimately than when traveling. We are loving others, very dear and important others, so we are happy. However, grandchildren grow up, perhaps go away to college, probably move to another town, and inevitably become so involved with their own lives that we are for them like an afterthought. And properly so. What then for us?

And there is of course denial. No matter how our neck sags or wrinkles, no matter how many lines run down our face, no matter how much our waist thickens, we can look into the mirror just so, at the proper angle, and see ourselves as we were five or ten years ago. Careful use of cosmetics and a well-styled coiffure work wonders for a woman. And a man can reassure himself by how much weight he can still lift or how fast he can mow the lawn. "I can do as much as I ever did." "You are only as old as you feel." "I still enjoy playing eighteen holes of golf, no problem." We have all heard these phrases, and perhaps we ourselves have said them, if not to others, then to ourselves.

So do we all need to think ahead about how we are to handle the challenges of old age? It seems not. There are indeed the lucky few, the people who sometime in their life have acquired a passion. It may be for music, painting, gardening, stamp collecting, horses, or any number of things. The more possible it is to pursue the passion late in life, the better. People with a passion, through some combination of inborn talents, personality traits, and well-used opportunities, discover themselves in old age almost by accident. Unless they become very ill or homebound, they may turn their heads, notice that they are old, and turn back to their passion, whatever it is. They may or may not discover the extra dimension of old age, but they do have natural protection from many of its challenges.

People with such driving passions are generally the creative ones of the world, those who are trying to make something fresh, bring a new order out of chaos, discover the heretofore unknown. They may be collectors, inventors, designers, craftsmen, artists, musicians, or who knows what else, but whatever their passion, they tend to pursue it as if it were their only purpose in life. They cannot leave it alone for long.

Watercolorist Barbara Ellis of Athol, Massachusetts, has completed more than a thousand listed paintings.
—photograph by Don Eaton

The arts are famous for people of passion. We think of musicians with a passion to compose, to conduct, or to play some instrument who simply continue doing what they have always done, but perhaps a little less of it as their bodies tire. Orchestra conductors have a reputation for sustaining their musical insight and physical vigour on the podium well into their eighties. Aging writers—not all, but those who cannot ever seem to leave it alone—find their way to their desks, typewriters, and computers when they have the energy to do little else. Painters look out their windows and return eagerly to their easels almost to the end of their lives. They are usually too busy creatively to give their old age much more than a passing nod.

I had the pleasure recently of visiting with one such artist, Barbara Ellis. A small, trim woman in her late eighties, Barbara lives in a charming house on a hill where Athol and Petersham, Massachusetts, intersect, overlooking endless mountains beneath a western sky. A perfect setting for an artist, in this case an accomplished watercolorist. In response to my several questions about successful aging, Barbara would pause, try to rearrange the question in her mind to fit some aspect of her experience, and politely express her puzzlement. After a bit of this and some broader conversation, I finally realized that she was a "person of passion." The beauty of the world, the challenge of translating some of this beauty onto paper, and the other people who share her passion—these three fill her life. And will undoubtedly continue to do so. She knows she will have to make some adaptations in her lifestyle and has already begun with a few changes, but without taking her eye off the art that still excites her.

Passions come in all shapes and sizes. I was privileged this past winter to interview Elsa Bakalar, the eighty-year-old author of the beautiful book entitled, *A Garden of One's Own: Making and Keeping Your Flower Garden.* Writing her book, published in 1994 when she was in her mid-seventies, was not a daunting venture for her, because writing had been a major part of the various jobs she had held since coming to America from her native England. Having skimmed her book, I expected to find a woman with a passion, but what I discovered was that she has not only one, but two.

The first—in time, at least—is teaching, and the second, gardening. For many years she taught English at various school levels and, after having discovered the gardening passion in midlife, she combined it with the teaching passion by lecturing and leading workshops in gardening. She has been very active in Greenfield's Community College, giving noncredit courses in many aspects of gardening to people of widely differing ages. And obviously enjoying every minute of it.

Elsa Bakalar of Ashfield, Massachusetts, considers design possibilities for her garden.
—photograph by Paul Franz

Elsa is of course aware that she and her husband are aging and that they may not always be as active as they are now. She is equally cognizant of there being less time left in her life, which she says has mellowed her a bit in her human relationships. But it is clear that her mind only turns to such thoughts occasionally. She is more interested in her gardens, lectures, and workshops. Will her passions carry her through more difficult times? I suspect they will, because she is already planning on how she can adapt—how she can pull back a little more from the physical demands of gardening and lecturing.

However, most of us are not "people of passion." We spend at least the first half of our lives in the work world earning a living, and at a certain age we are usually forced or choose to leave that world and enter the one of retirement. We have our hobbies and our sports, some of which can stir our minds and hold our enthusiasm when our bodies begin to give out, but many of which cannot. This is when we need to pause and look ahead, because there are challenges to be faced, particularly if we become ill or unable for one reason or another to leave our homes.

This time of life brings to mind several similes. The most obvious one concerns exam time in a school or college. The student knows that exam time—like old age—is ahead. Some students just drift through classes and assignments, barely passing tests, and talking with their classmates about how awful the exams may be, way into the future. Others keep their eyes on the next test and prepare for that alone, as if no exam were to come. Still others wisely hold in the back of their minds that the examination at the end of the school year is what really counts. These last experience the special thrill of writing an examination for which they have prepared well. The others may feel considerable regret upon opening the exam book, saying, "Oh, no. I should have known this question would be here. I should have prepared for this."

Another more complex simile involves canoeing. Picture a large lake, with a stream running down from it, full of rocks and stones and therefore of rapids of all sorts. Now add a young man who has parked at the foot of the stream. Glancing at the rough waters alongside the path but thinking primarily of the beautiful lake upstream, he walks along a path up to the lake. Here he has rented a canoe, with any luck a well-made one. He gets his paddle and begins to canoe happily round and round the lake, sometimes paddling easily on a placid surface, sometimes drifting along the shoreline, and at still other times contending with wind and waves. He notes the outlet into the stream and casually observes the other canoeists starting down it, on their way to the dropoff point for the canoes. He knows that he too must enter this stream. Finally he does, and sees whitewater up ahead.

At this point, the intelligent and experienced canoeist does not panic and just head straight into the stream, hoping that luck will get him through to the end. Instead, he pulls to shore, climbs to a high point, observes the water up ahead, and carefully plans his descent down the rapids. He figures out which side of which rock will keep him in the main current without scraping or upsetting the canoe. He looks for the next vantage point where he can again pull over to survey even further down the stream. He prepares, so that he can successfully meet the challenges ahead. If he has become a good canoeist, he may view this as the best part of the trip, the time when his skills are sharpened and tested, marking his development into an expert canoeist.

For us, the examination is up ahead, as are the rapids, both unavoidable. Just as the student and the canoeist are foolish to deny or ignore the future, so are we foolish to think we can avoid it by acting as if we were young, refusing to think about our aging, or doing anything we can to keep ourselves from acknowledging it. We would be wise to look toward the future and see what it may hold for us. Doing so may reveal nothing more fearful than the examination to the good student or the rapids to the experienced canoeist.

Viewing Old Age as a New Stage of Growth

All the authors I have read agree that fear of aging is destructive, and that we should view it not only as a challenge but also as an opportunity, difficult as that may sometimes be, even remembering its possible joys and rewards. It is a time for growth.

"What grows never grows old,"

[Noah benShea, *Oxford*, p. 67]

as Noah benShea's character Jacob appraises the situation.

Betty Friedan's theme in *The Fountain of Age* is that, difficult though it may be, we should acknowledge our aging and face it as an opportunity for growth. Two of the most concise statements, however, occur in articles she wrote about her book for two national magazines.

The problem is, first of all, how to break through the cocoon of our illusory youth and risk a new stage in life, where there are no prescribed roles, no models, no guideposts, no rigid rules or visible rewards—how to step out into the true existential unknown of these years of life now open to us and to find our own terms for living them.

[Friedan, *Time*, September 6, 1993, p. 62]

It's only when we break through that desperate denial of age that we can begin to sense the new possibilities of continued growth and development after 30, after 50, even after 70—the new adventures of mind, body and spirit we might be free to risk, the new ways of loving, living and working that can open when we are liberated from some of the things that drove us and held us back in our youth.

[Friedan, *Parade*, March 20, 1994, p. 4]

Poet Stanley Kunitz believes the self confidence that can come from experience may lead us to take risks:

In a curious way I think that with age comes a diminishing of barriers. You can take greater risks at a certain point because you don't care anymore. You've tested yourself, you know what you can do, you know better than anyone else and who's to stop you from daring to do something that is not expected from you?

[Kunitz, *Ageless*, p. 135]

Aging is a part of our natural growth process. Dr. Bortz tells about how his father, also a doctor, handled a patient's question about preventing aging by responding,

"I'm not interested in arrested development."

[Bortz, p. 3]

Like his father, Dr. Bortz sees age as a stage of life in which there should continue to be further development of the human being. Even when we enter the later years of extremely limited activity, there may be some development beyond, a spiritual growth that is difficult to describe but hinted at by many authors. Scott-Maxwell puts it this way,

> Here we come to a new place of which I knew nothing. We come to where age is boring, one's interest in it by-passed; further on, go further on, one finds that one has arrived at a larger place still, the place of release. There one says, "Age can seem a debacle, a rout of all one most needs, but that is not the whole truth. What of the part of us, the nameless, boundless part who experienced the rout, the witness who saw so much go, who remains undaunted and knows with clear conviction that there is more to us than age? . . . If we have suffered defeat we are somewhere, somehow beyond the battle".
>
> [Scott-Maxwell, pp. 140-41]

Preparing for Old Age

Many books about old people who are considered successful agree on basic ingredients, most of which depend on attitudes and practices developed long before we reach old age. It behooves us to prepare while we can. And we are not without guides—physicians, psychologists, columnists, novelists, and others.

Dr. Hallowell emphasizes the necessity to prepare for old age.

> Study after study and interview after interview with those who are happy and relatively healthy in their later years come up with the same conclusions—aging must be prepared for. Those who ignore its approach or who let it sneak up are going to be thrown off balance.
>
> [Hallowell, p. 26]

Harton, in her book specifically on the subject of preparing for old age, writes,

> Preparation for old age may mean the adoption and the cultivation of a new mental and spiritual outlook, which obviously must claim our attention long before the end, and the middle years are not too early to begin it.
>
> [Harton, p. 7, in the foreword]

Fisher also points out that, because aging is simply another stage of life, it requires the same amount of preparation that we give the earlier stages. She writes that

> this steady fading away . . . is viewed with alarm and is generally found unacceptable, when really it is the natural thing and is symptomatic of nothing at alll.
>
> [Fisher, *Last House*, p. 273]

Fortunately, though, because I met Sister Age so long ago, I can watch my own aging with a detachment she has taught me. I know about the dismays and delights of my condition, and wish that all of us could prepare ourselves for them as instinctively and with as much outside help as we do those of puberty, adolescence, pregnancy, menopausal and climacteric changes.

[Fisher, "Afterword" in *Sister* Age, p. 235]

Dr. Hallowell helps us to approach our aging optimistically with his assessment of the increasing social acceptance of older people, particularly if they remain in good health.

It is fair to say that this is the most exciting time to be growing old that the world has ever witnessed. . . . Being old is increasingly more a state of mind than a biological marker. Those over sixty-five are no longer so readily looked down upon for being elderly unless they fulfill the stereotypical image—frail, retiring, forgetful and in poor health. These misfortunes occur to fewer and fewer people in their sixties and seventies and are increasingly becoming the burden of the so called "old old," those over eighty-five.

[Hallowell, p. 268]

Dr. Hallowell even goes a step further than social acceptance for the old.

Yet we have far more control over our aging than we thought possible even five years ago. Americans are beginning to realize the potential grace, even the elegance, of being old. Within us, we harbor an image of the ideal old—a sharp-boned, quick-minded, glistening-eyed soul whose compassion, wisdom and independence of thought beckon and caress us. It is the grandparent image. . . .

[Hallowell, p. 19]

This chapter looks at ways to prepare for a "successful" old age. High on the list is doing all we can to prevent physical disabilities, since we must first live long enough to reach old age.

Maintaining Physical Health

Dr. Hallowell's book, *Growing Old, Staying Young*, provides detailed discussion of exercise and diet in a very readable form. Dr. Bortz, in his optimistic *We Live Too Short and Die Too Long: How to Achieve and Enjoy Your Natural 100-Year-Plus Life Span*, gives much the same advice. To maintain physical health, both doctors advise regular aerobic exercise, a proper diet, and sufficient sleep. Just what our mothers told us and what we read in newspapers and magazines every day, with their increased emphasis on vitamins and herbs in our diets. The hitch, of course, is that few of us begin to follow this advice as early as we should. Often we are into late middle life, glancing askance at the approach of disabilities, before we figure we had better do something about maintaining our health.

Dr. Bortz stresses the importance of preventing illness and the simplicity of the formula.

Prevention is low theater, low visibility, low interest, low investment, and low commitment.

Prevention is health; and health is the combination of our three basic ingredients—*plus* not doing anything to hurt yourself.

[Bortz, p. 74]

He quotes René Dubos, who wrote:

"Health can be earned only by a disciplined way of life."

[Bortz, p. 184]

Discipline may be most necessary in order to assure ourselves of sufficient exercise. Dr. Hallowell emphasizes its importance. Speaking first of medical insurance coverage, he writes,

the best coverage comes from the benefits of years of exercise before and after retirement. . . . Exercise to keep the cardiovascular system as young as possible, to keep joints flexible, muscles in shape and endurance up is really an inexpensive form of preventive medicine.

[Hallowell, p. 241]

Dr. Bortz emphasizes exercise for psychological as well as physical reasons.

Exercise confers a quality of sangfroid—imperturbability, equanimity, and lack of urgency. Action allays anxiety. Exercise is the balance wheel to tension.

[Bortz, p. 192]

And also for physical reasons:

To obtain a conditioning effect, a person must exercise three times a week for half an hour per session at a consistent intensity.

[Bortz, p. 195]

He lists the same elements of successful aging as several researchers. At Duke University, a longitudinal study of 268 subjects proposed four elements: work satisfaction, happiness, good health, and not smoking. Erik and Joan Erikson, in *Vital Involvement in Old Age*, deduced from their research that what they term "generativity" is the key to success. By this they mean a type of involvement that is "taking care of what is being procreated, produced, and created." They found that all twenty-nine elders they studied in depth had a

"near religious faith in industriousness and competence."

[Bortz, p. 222]

Dr. Bortz adds a sense of control:

The importance of a sense of control to overall health increases as we age, because advancing age, despite all counteractive strategies, inevitably involves deteriorations and threatening change.

[Bortz, p. 225]

He also reports on interviews with twelve hundred centenarians recorded and summarized in *Living To Be 100* by Osborne Segerberg:

Ninety-six percent of the responses reflected a high degree of order in their lives. . . . Next in the list of characteristics was stability—these people didn't often move their households; and the third characteristic was a strong family fabric.

[Bortz, p. 234]

Segerberg concluded that

> will is not simply another trait in the centenarians' repertoire, but the centerpiece.
>
> [Bortz, p. 235]

Another survey, this one of a hundred centenarians by Dr. Belle Boone Beard, a sociologist at the University of Georgia, concluded that

> their central identifying feature was "an exceptional ability to make social adjustment." Their sense of harmony and absence of frustration were notable.
>
> [Bortz, p. 235]

Obviously most of the studies of successful aging quoted above involve not only physical but behavioral and social elements, the latter two being major contributors to health in old age. The elements prescribed by them all are

- aerobic exercise, proper diet, sufficient sleep
- involvement in life, industry
- sense of control, orderly life, will, stability
- strong family fabric, ability to adjust socially

Recent and authoritative prescriptions for aging well appear in a book entitled *Successful Aging*, written by Dr. John W. Rowe and Dr. Robert L. Kahn under the aegis of the MacArthur Foundation. Their ten years of research among thousands of elderly people confirm previous findings. The authors recommend "forward-looking, active engagement with life and other human beings," remaining productive, and especially establishing healthful habits, with an emphasis on exercise. They found that such practices determine seventy percent of the mental and physical attributes of people sixty-five to seventy-five and even a higher percentage for those in their eighties. The book also points out the great progress that has already been made in decreasing disability among the elderly.

All the recommended elements—physical, behavioral, and social—are at work in the life of a North Orange writer whom I was privileged to interview. Charlotte Ryan is in her mid-eighties, but she has the body, both in appearance and ability, of a woman in her forties who has kept herself in good condition. Not only is she slim without the skinniness often witnessed in older people, but she regularly mows her own lawn, climbs a ladder to trim her bushes, and cuts and piles firewood. She laughingly complains that she can no longer jump rope. She admits to having inherited good genes, pointing to close relatives in the former generation who lived into their nineties and beyond.

Genes alone are not responsible for Charlotte's exceptional physical condition. She has been active physically, mentally, and socially all her life. Possessing an athletic body, she reached high skill levels in sailing, skiing, and horseback riding. Her keen interest and ability in the study of history, primarily relating to educa-

Charlotte Ryan of North Orange, Massachusetts, welcomes her dog Friedman to her study after a morning spent writing and reviewing educational documents.

tion and its relationship to politics, led her into responsible jobs for the nation, state, and community. She is currently writing a scholarly work on the history of education and polity and is actively involved in day-to-day workings of the region's educational system.

Charlotte's life has not been without stress. Ten years ago her husband of fifty years died. Three years ago one of her four children, a son, died. She has also lost a brother in the last few years. Another son who is living with her is far from well. She herself has apparently had few serious illnesses since childhood, and she is very casual about the skin cancers that have only temporarily cramped her style by taking precious time from her writing and community commitments. When I asked her how she handled these difficulties, her chin lifted just a trifle and, while admitting the trauma of the deaths, said that she keeps on writing and working outside. She paused, and then she said that after she had turned eighty, she was advised to start "taking it easy." Which she says she did for a period. And then that she came to her senses and went back to her regular physical exertions. Her belief is that, as you age, you should just keep on doing everything you want and need to do just as long as you can.

Charlotte also offered three specific bits of advice for people who are along in years. They all fall under her admonition, "Pay attention." The first is to "stay over your feet," to help one's balance, which may not be as good as previously. The second is to avoid getting chilled, which she has noted is apt to lead to serious colds more easily than in earlier years. And the third is to "pay attention" when someone is speaking, avoiding the tendency to muse that I noted earlier as one of the appropriate developments of aging. These represent some of Charlotte's ways of adapting to the physical changes of later years.

Even those of us with less exceptional genes than Charlotte's can still greatly affect our health for the better, and in many of the same ways as she has. LeShan puts it this way:

> Even in old age, self-healing still takes place. Best if there is little anxiety and stress; best if we have interesting and useful lives; best if we feel loved and can love others. There is every evidence that self-healing is most powerful in those who want to live the most. When we bring this power to the battle for wellness it can make an enormous difference at any age.
>
> [LeShan, *50 Again*, p. 135]

Nevertheless, it must also be said that a careful look at what may happen to us if we do not take proper care of all aspects of our health may perhaps inspire us to do so. LeShan, after many interviews with the aging, put the need to maintain one's health very bluntly:

> Every single person with whom I discussed aging said that health was the keystone—health was the difference between a bearable or an unbearable old age.
>
> [LeShan, *50 Again*, p. 129]

Let us look first at the "unbearable," the darker side of old age where lie the greatest challenges—at worst, pain; at best, eventual disabilities.

Facing Physical Challenges

The elderly whom I have known well have dealt in very individual ways with the physical challenges they have faced. I admit, of course, to guessing what each has been going through, aware always that I am seeing only a fraction of the situation. The only generalization that holds for everyone is that disabilities are met at first by an attempt to carry on as usual. This might be called courage, but is most often called denial. I think it is both, and that it is a healthy response. In most cases, where the disability or pain is permanent, the progression follows quite nearly that of dying—denial, anger, bargaining, depression, and acceptance. I have not been aware of "bargaining" by any of the elderly I visit, but perhaps it was left unspoken.

Accepting the Challenges

The least accepting of her disabilities has been Margaret. Only in her early sixties, she has become increasingly blind over the past four years and has been diabetic for about fifteen. She is divorced, overweight, and living by herself in a trailer. At present she is denying, angry, and depressed, separately and all together. She is out there fighting. My word for her is "gutsy." In many ways, but not all, she still tries to carry on as if she were not "visually impaired," a term she still prefers to "blind." For example, she displays dozens of knickknacks on her tables and other surfaces, which she changes with the season, instead of clearing the surfaces so she will not knock things over—as she does.

On the other hand, Margaret is adapting by taking many practical steps. She writes with a thick magic marker on large white surfaces. She has edged the white steps leading to her trailer with red paint. She uses equipment especially adapted for the blind, such as telephone, sunglasses, and audiocassettes. She takes advantage of transportation for the elderly to allow her to attend support groups and senior center meals. Most importantly, she has not lost her sense of humor. She loves to kid and be kidded, even about mistakes her blindness causes.

Unfortunately, she can turn very fast from humor to anger, if one of the people trying to help her does something she considers stupid or thoughtless. Such occurrences frustrate her, because she knows if she could see she could do it all so much better and so much faster. Unfortunately, she seems to feel that she is owed something by other people because she is blind. All in all, however, she is adapting very well despite her denial and anger. I wonder whether in time she will be able to accept. She could swing either way.

Most accepting of all is Ella, the frail farm woman I mentioned earlier with a quote about dying. I only knew her for the last six months of her life, so perhaps I simply missed the earlier stages. She was not only eighty-five, blind, and dying of emphysema, but also had completely lost her ability to remember anything about recent times. Whenever I arrived, she was sitting at a grease-stained table in a tiny, messy little kitchen, sipping a cup of horrible cold coffee. I know it was horrible, because I once made the mistake of accepting a cup. In spite of emphysema, she always had a few cigarette stubs in the ash trays, perhaps left over from the day before, perhaps smoked that morning. If anyone else was there besides me, she would turn her gaze downward and seem to be elsewhere in her thoughts. Not unhappy, just not involving herself in whatever small talk was taking place.

However, when others left and there were just the two of us, Ella lifted her head, seemed to look toward me with her soft blue eyes, and positively bloomed as she spoke. I asked her questions about old times, and she told me about cleaning three houses every week, about how chunks of ice were cut and brought to the house, and about her husband and children when they were young.

Ella had not lost her sense of humor, which at times seemed a surprisingly naughty one. For example, she laughingly told me that her sister-in-law's mother said that the sister-in-law was a "rotten daughter." This amused her highly. At other times, she expressed amusement at her own disabilities. I brought her some audio books, which she said she enjoyed, noting that I could bring her the same ones all over again, because she had already forgotten everything she had heard.

What amazed me was that Ella did not seem unhappy. She only complained once, but that was in the context of having had visitors, which she said made her tired, adding that it was better than being bored, however. When I asked her directly why she seemed so content, she paused and then answered straightforwardly, saying that her mother had really loved and "enjoyed" her (her wit, I believe), that she was living with a son who loved and cared for her, and that her husband had also loved her. She had told me many times that he had often said that she was "the most wonderful woman" he had ever met, and there was no one like her. As for her memory, she said that everyone forgets things, and that she still "thought" well—which was true. She often remarked that a person needs to do the best she can do, not the best that someone else can do. Ella had accepted her blindness, emphysema, and memory loss; she felt loved—past and present— and she was content.

I will give one more example of how the elderly women I visit have reacted to their disabilities and pain. Elaine was different from the rest. She simply never spoke to me of physical problems, much less complained. Elaine was a handsome lady in her mid-eighties. She thoroughly enjoyed our excursions every Wednesday noon. We might do an errand or two, but the pièce de résistance was our luncheon, and together we explored just about every diner and other eating place within an hour's radius, feeling at times like two very daring and naughty ladies. It was absolutely necessary to her as a matter of pride that she think of me as her "friend," not just an agency's volunteer.

Over the time that I saw Elaine, she deteriorated from walking with little help and eating heartily to being able to go only occasionally, walking with her arm over mine, and nibbling at her food. Aware that she was experiencing some sort of intestinal illness, I once remarked to her that I seemed to be the only one complaining of any physical problem. I had neck difficulties at the time. I hoped to bring her out a bit and give her a chance to talk about her situation. Just about every other older person would have jumped at the opportunity to complain awhile. Elaine, however, just smiled—rather smugly in fact—and in effect politely declined to open up.

Eventually, she went for exploratory surgery, stayed in the hospital for several weeks, and then spent her last six months in a nursing home. Everyone there loved her for her graciousness and consideration. Although I visited with her throughout this time, she passed off all opportunities to talk about her illness or pain. She always greeted me warmly but made it clear that she preferred to hear about my animals, my husband, anything in my life. I suspect that this reticence was not confined to me. She was just that way, before and after her illness. She had chosen to forego the relief of complaint in order to glean some pleasure from ordinary human intercourse and to retain her own self-esteem and sense of herself as a person. I think of her often as I drive past our various luncheon "haunts" and miss her, because she had very definitely become my friend.

Despite natural differences in how each person handles pain or disabilities, there may be some guidelines to be gleaned from those who have thought and felt strongly enough on the subject to write about it.

Living through Pain

The Western medical profession has been giving increased attention to pain relief, particularly for the very old or the dying. And, of course, techniques for ignoring or transforming pain have been prevalent throughout the ages, particularly in Eastern practice. Nevertheless, many and perhaps most of us will have to endure pain of some degree and substantial length before we are through, so some discussion of the psychological aspect of handling pain is still relevant.

Sarton describes her reactions to illness and pain in several journals. After the age of sixty-six, she had to face a mastectomy, a stroke, and a long bout with lung cancer. She pulls no punches about her frailty and pain, as well as the depression, frustration, and loneliness it brought. She says that she feels

so ill and frail all the time it is not a real life anymore.

[Sarton, *Endgame*, p. 23]

The following were written when she was seventy-nine and eighty years old.

Depression comes from impotence. It's irritating not to be able to walk a straight line, but to fumble, as I walk, to stumble is what I mean, to almost fall so often, and to feel extremely tired and begin to pant if I walk even twenty yards.

[Sarton, *Endgame*, p. 67]

I feel terribly lonely. It's not a loneliness for a single person; it's not wanting somebody to come and see me; it's loneliness from a feeling of helplessness—that I can't handle so much pain.

[Sarton, *Endgame*, p. 141]

I want to die, there's no doubt about that. When you have as much pain as I have and there's no way out you do want to die, if you're as old as I am. You do want to die. There is that hope that someday, while you're asleep, the old heart will stop beating.

[Sarton, *Endgame*, pp. 277-78]

Sarton offers endurance and hope, which she expresses as "trying to believe that someday I can get better." And in fact, she shows an incredible amount of hope throughout her journals, more hope than seems reasonable to the reader. Whenever she has a good day, she seems to think that she is on the verge of being cured.

Scott-Maxwell at eighty-three also wrote of pain and the loneliness of it.

Disabilities crowd in on the old; real pain is there, and if we have to be falsely cheerful, it is part of our isolation.

[Scott-Maxwell, p. 32]

Several times she advises that when life is at its worst, one must "wait," implying a combination of Sarton's endurance and hope.

When old, one has only one's soul as company. There are times when you can feel it crying, you do not ask why. Your eyes are dry, but heavy, hot tears drop on your heart. There is nothing to do but wait, and listen to the emptiness which is sometimes gentle. You and the day are quiet, and you have no comment to make.

[Scott-Maxwell, pp. 119-20]

The crucial task of age is balance, a veritable tight-rope of balance; keeping just well enough, just brave enough, just gay and interested and starkly honest enough to remain a sentient human being. On the day when we can boast none of this, we must be able to wait until the balance is restored. When we sink to nothingness we must remember that only yesterday our love was warm.

[Scott-Maxwell, p. 36]

Unlike Sarton, however, Scott-Maxwell speaks of an unexplained influx of strength after an earlier fractured femur and then another operation:

Then strength arrived and forced me to recognize that just because this accident had happened I was stronger. Where the strength and the will to use it had come from I could not imagine, but who understands the ebb and flow of energy? At first I did not believe in this new strength, but it was there, vital, mine. Now after the operation some new life was near.

[Scott-Maxwell, p. 93]

When truly old, too frail to use the vigour that pulses in us, and weary, sometimes even scornful of what can seem the pointless activity of mankind, we may sink down to some deeper level and find a new supply of life that amazes us.

[Scott-Maxwell, p. 139]

Harton suggests a distinctly spiritual and religious response to pain that involves "relaxing into it," reminiscent of Eastern practice and certain modern adaptations.

To brace oneself against pain, to fight it by refusal, to try to beat it down, may quite well increase its power and reduce the sufferer's capacity to bear it; a better way of meeting it may be to relax oneself into it, or beneath it, as it were, to swim with or in it rather than against it, and after it reaches a pitch which may seem unbearable, the pain's intensity gradually diminishes, until by contrast it is almost relief.

[Harton, pp. 78-79]

A few pages earlier, Harton puts forth a fascinating possibility concerning that baffling condition of senility and imbecility which may attend old age.

[Harton, p. 73]

I quote her at length to give this difficult concept concerning dementia and semi-consciousness the full force and scope that is missing if it is cut substantially.

We simply do not know what is or may be going on in the depths of the spirit when mind and senses are withdrawn from normal reactions. If you have attended a death-bed when the dying one has lain for weeks immobile in a state of semi-consciousness or even less, you may, in the rare times of returning consciousness, have been allowed to see that, far from being dormant like the body, the spirit has been responding to some purifying, renewing force, so that it reveals, though with a greatly reduced power of expression, a new goodness, a new nobility. It is certain that a withdrawn self can undergo deep subjective experiences during a period of mental quiescence, and more may be accomplished than we can understand. All nature grows in the dark, and it is God's providence which ordains who it is who needs that darkness of mind and sense in which the spirit can fulfil its final consummation. We do not know at what perfection they are inwardly gazing, who endure this strange state of senile decay.

[Harton, p. 74]

The final rescuer of course is death, as Vining notes, only in her seventieth year and thus a bit more lightly:

When an individual has too much to bear, he is eased by death, which comes as a friend. And no one's life is wholly pain; each has some moments of beauty, of happiness.

[Vining, p. 168]

Stanley Kunitz, at the age of eighty-six, wrote the following poem after the death of a friend. I feel it grasps the contradictory experiences that may be implicit as one approaches death.

The Long Boat

When his boat snapped loose
from its moorings, under
the screaking of the gulls,
he tried at first to wave
to his dear ones on shore,
but in the rolling fog
they had already lost their faces.
Too tired even to choose
between jumping and calling,
somehow he felt absolved and free
of his burdens, those mottoes
stamped on his name-tag:
conscience, ambition, and all
that caring.
He was content to lie down
with the family ghosts
in the slop of his cradle,
buffeted by the storm,
endlessly drifting.
Peace, Peace!
To be rocked by the Infinite
As if it didn't matter
which way was home;
as if it didn't know
he loved the earth so much
he wanted to stay forever.

[Kunitz, *Ageless*, pp. 136-37]

Handling Disabilities

Even if we maintain our health as well as we can and are lucky enough to be spared serious illness and sustained acute pain, our bodies will gradually wear out bit by bit. One or another disability will occur and we will become increasingly frail. Even this is being debated today, however. In "Toward a Natural History of Aging," John Lauerman writes, after surveying various studies:

Although aging certainly is accompanied by change in capacity, it's not clear that age imposes illness or frailty, as has been so commonly assumed.

[Lauerman, *Harvard Magazine*, p. 61]

Any discussion of the disabilities of old age should begin with the acknowledgment that they can be a formidable challenge to the spirit. Fisher, in one of her essays in *Last House*, describes vividly how she was feeling in her eightieth year, after a fall had badly bruised her ribs:

I really am very ready to stop going through the increasingly difficult motions of being an upright human person. I would like to lie down and not move again. I do not want to eat, or drink, ever again. I hate the thought that soon I must stand up carefully, turn slowly so that I do not stagger or trip, and walk into the other room and eat something and listen to the radio and then turn out the lights and come carefully and slowly in to undress and get into bed. What I want to do is go straight to my bed, and lie cautiously down between two small pillows I have fixed so that my ribs do not hurt, and pull up my cover and lie in the dark. I am not sleepy. But I am tired. I think it may be time for me to die. Why not? . . . In other words, I am conditioned to living as decently as possible while I have to. By now, it is a chore.

[Fisher, *Last House*, pp. 232-33]

Actually, she lived four more years, and during the next year writes far more positively about her aging.

I honestly do feel that anyone who can live decently, or even with some difficulty into and past middle age, and then attain old age is lucky. He is *fortunate*.

[Fisher, *Last House*, p. 275]

Scott-Maxwell describes her problems with increasing physical disabilities and her ever-present awareness of the approach of death.

We old people are short tempered because we suffer so. We are stretched too far, our gamut is painfully wide. Little things have become big; nothing in us works well, our bodies have become unreliable. We have to make an effort to do the simplest things. We urge now this, now that part of our flagging bodies, and when we have spurred them to further functioning we feel clever and carefree. We stretch from such concerns as these into eternity where we keep one eye on death, certain of continuity, then uncertain, then indifferent.

[Scott-Maxwell, p. 35]

LeShan, typically realistic, states baldly,

Any kind of physical incapacity or illness interferes with the person we have been, changes our sense of identity.

[LeShan, *50 Again*, p. 131]

And how are we to face these difficult changes? A good summary is offered by Fisher.

What is important, though, is that our dispassionate acceptance of attrition be matched by a full use of everything that has ever happened in all the long wonderful-ghastly years to free a person's mind from his body . . . to use the experience, both great and evil, so that physical annoyances are surmountable in an alert and even mirthful appreciation of life itself.

[Fisher, *Sister Age*, p. 237]

Almost all the authors' advice seems to be to face age straight on as a challenge, looking for the bright side. Skinner puts it this way.

Attack old age as a problem to be solved. . . . Instead of complaining of the sere, the yellow leaf, you can enjoy the autumn foliage. Instead of learning to bear the taste of bitter fruit, you can squeeze that last sweet drop of juice from the orange.

[Skinner, p. 24]

Cowley says much the same thing in his own vigorous way, and then shortly supplies an amusing quotation.

I sympathize with their problems, but the men and women I envy are those who accept old age as a series of challenges.

For such persons, every new infirmity is an enemy to be outwitted, an obstacle to be overcome by force of will. They enjoy each little victory over themselves, and sometimes they win a major success.

[Cowley, p. 16]

"Eighty years old!" the great Catholic poet Paul Claudel wrote in his journal. "No eyes left, no ears, no teeth, no legs, no wind! And when all is said and done, how astonishingly well one does without them!"

[Cowley, p. 17]

The attraction of a challenge is expressed vividly by Grandpa in *Cold Sassy Tree* by Olive Ann Burns.

And I found out long time ago, when I look on what I got to stand as a dang hardship or a burden, it seems too heavy to carry. But when I look on the same dang thang as a challenge, why, standin' it or acceptin' it is like you done entered a contest. Hit even gits excitin', waitin' to see how everthan's go'n turn out."

[Burns, *Oxford*, pp. 314-15]

For Cowley also, a courageous acceptance of the challenge of old age seems to be his primary way of dealing with it.

Seventy-year olds, or septuas, have the illusion of being middle-aged, even if they have been pushed back on a shelf. The 80-year old, the octo, looks at the double-dumpling figure and admits that he is old. The last act has begun, and it will be the test of the play.

[Cowley, p. 2]

In his new role the old person will find that he is tempted by new vices, that he receives new compensations (not so widely known), and that he may possibly achieve new virtues. Chief among these is the heroic or merely obstinate refusal to surrender in the face of time. One admires the ships that go down with all flags flying and the captain on the bridge.

[Cowley, p. 8]

Courage is also emphasized by Phillip Berman in his introduction to the anthology, *The Ageless Spirit*.

This business about living, this business about moving through the world with vitality and zest and humor and joy, is about courage. It is about the courage to look at your life with honesty and to take the necessary steps—at any age, on any stage—to brighten the world around you. As the men and women who speak within these pages so readily show, the obstacles we face are nothing more than opportunities to learn about our latent potentialities.

[Berman, *Ageless*, p. 12]

Harton provides some perspective on the need for fortitude in this succinct statement.

As we look ahead we can make up our minds that old age with its declining powers requires fortitude; but so does any age.

[Harton, p. 106]

The comparison that both Berman and Harton make with earlier years is also made by the German novelist, Hermann Hesse, who emphasizes affirmation rather than fortitude.

To put it briefly, to fulfill the meaning of age and to perform its duty one must be reconciled with old age and everything it brings with it. One must say yes to it. Without this yea, without submission to what nature demands of us, the worth and meaning of our days—whether we are old or young—are lost and we betray life.

[Hesse, *Oxford*, p. 56]

I particularly liked Scott-Maxwell's very autobiographical picture of how she reacts when still one more serious ache or pain occurs.

When a new disability arrives I look about to see if death has come, and I call quietly, "Death, is that you? Are you there?". So far the disability has answered, "Don't be silly, it's me."

[Scott-Maxwell, p. 36]

Light-heartedness about disabilities and death is important for several authors. Vining writes,

When we were in our thirties, my friend Marjorie and I used to classify old ladies in four categories. We said there were the Whiny Old Ladies, the Bossy Old Ladies, the Fussy Old Ladies, and the Batty Old Ladies. I decided that if I lived so long—which I did not intend to do—I would be a Batty Old Lady. Well, I am.

[Vining, p. 30]

And you will remember the earlier humorous quotations by Beatrice Wood, who saw herself in the mirror as a horse, and by Florida Scott-Maxwell, who danced in the kitchen by herself. All these approaches indicate the value of humor, which is after all a result of gaining some perspective on ourselves, a possible gift of aging.

Some of the creative persons interviewed for *The Ageless Spirit* in fact seem to value humor even above courage. For example, actor Ossie Davis says,

I would say life comes a lot easier if you maintain your sense of humor, no matter how old you are. I believe that humor is divine; it's one of God's greatest gifts to us. It enables us to put things into perspective and to understand that we are very large and yet also very small, and to make adjustment, one with the other.

[Davis, *Ageless*, p. 63]

Radio and television broadcaster Art Linkletter, not surprisingly, agrees.

In all of this, humor is the lubricant you need to get through life, and it is particularly important as you age. If you can't laugh at your wrinkles and aches, you've got to scream. And poking fun at problems is the basis of a great deal of humor.

[Linkletter, *Ageless*, p. 171]

Actor Jason Robards uses a different metaphor for the same thought.

Humor has a way of lightening the load, and I'm finding that it is becoming more and more important to me as I grow older.

[Robards, *Ageless*, p. 224]

I have found that humor has indeed lightened the load for some of my clients. This is particularly true of Susan, who at eighty-two has recently lost much of her eyesight to macular degeneration. She also has difficulty walking. More importantly, her husband died only a year ago, and two years ago her son was killed in an automobile accident. After their deaths, she moved from her home in Michigan to live in Greenfield in a comfortable apartment next door to her daughter and son-in-law. A former school teacher, she is an intelligent and sociable person. She knew that she needed to get out and meet other people, so she eagerly accepted the offer of a "companion" from the home care agency.

Shortly after I arrived at Susan's door, we decided we were a perfect match. She showed me how she walked, making fun of herself. I joined in, and we had our first good laugh. Since then, any little thing that can be the slightest cause for humor starts us off laughing. Even such little things as her trouble fastening the seat belt in my car. Many times she simply talks about her problems and pains as one friend to another, but always there is a possibility for a laugh in between. The result is a much happier Susan after our two hours together. And I will admit that I usually feel pretty good, too.

Humor and courage in the face of challenge are a beginning. But then, given this positive attitude, what do we actually do in response to our aging and all that it means?

Adapting, Changing, and Choosing

If we view old age, disabilities and all, as a challenge, we are assuming that we have power to do something about how it affects us—that we have choices. This may sound obvious, but I have noticed that some older people, weary and ill, quite understandably give up too soon when a new disability arrives, saying to themselves, "Now that this has happened, I know I am really old and will just have to sit here and wait for death. There is nothing I can do about it." The authors I have read agree that acceptance of the situation is important, but we must not stop there. We must adapt.

Eda LeShan typically puts the first step succinctly.

> A pretty good summary of what we need most as we get older: to hold on to what gives us the greatest pleasure, and to do so while accepting the need for eventually slowing down. For many of us this may be one of the hardest tasks we've ever faced, and most of us come to the choices we have to make with little or no preparation.
>
> [LeShan, *50 Again*, p. 83]

Quoting Kenneth Minaker of Harvard Medical School, John Lauerman in an article about aging writes about the necessity and the ability of many aging people to adapt to physical changes.

> "There's a tendency to muddle through. . . . I think that advancing age means adapting to limits on maximum capacities that allow people to adjust, but without doing self-damage. Physiologically, age is a time of adaptation, when compensatory mechanisms adjust in order to fight off challenges and keep self-regulated. You can't tolerate severe challenges, but for little hits you manage pretty well."
>
> [Lauerman, *Harvard Magazine*, p. 63]

LeShan takes her advice of acceptance a big step forward, by suggesting it be followed by exercising control over our lives.

> Once we have accepted the ambiguous feelings of aging, once we have acknowledged the changes in the world inside ourselves—once we are fully engaged in the search for our fullest identity—we are ready to move on, to use our powers, to make choices, to control our lives for all the future we may have at our disposal.
>
> [LeShan, *50 Again*, p. 82]

Friedan states the importance of remaining flexible.

> Continued choice and control over your life require openness and flexibility.
>
> [Friedan, *Parade Magazine*, p. 5]

LeShan also speaks of flexibility, with a wry turn at the end.

> Flexibility seems to be the name of the game. We need to learn that it is important to keep our options open. We have to accept changes we can't do anything about—but we don't have to like all of them.
>
> [LeShan, *50 Again*, p. 49]

Recognizing the opportunity to do something new is a major point for LeShan.

> Learning *not* to do things we don't love anymore is an important way to use our opportunities for change.
>
> [LeShan, *50 Again*, p. 50]

Not a chance that the five-pound lobster would fit into the two-pound lobster's shell!
—photograph courtesy of Today's Catch, Athol, Massachusetts

She emphasizes the point with an amusing comparison.

> Trying to stay the same, remain the same person, no matter what is happening, is like becoming a five-pound lobster trying to survive in a two-pound lobster's shell—suffocating, desperate, impossible.
>
> [LeShan, *50 Again*, p. 58]

She refers again to the lobster analogy in an interview, in which she points to the need for courage and humor.

> You know, if you stay stifled where you are, you're dead before you're dead. So the thing you need more than anything else when you get old is the courage of the lobster. You are going to go through things where you have to become much more flexible. You have to be willing to change, you have to face painful crisis, and courage is absolutely the most essential part of it. Courage and a sense of humor, that's what you need.
>
> [LeShan, *Ageless*, pp. 152-53]

Throughout her book on aging, *Oh, To Be 50 Again*, LeShan emphasizes optimistic flexibility and also creativity as major keys to success in aging.

> The tasks are different from any we have met with in the past, but they are similar in one important respect; as in all the other stages of our lives, we can make some choices. Whether our circumstances at any given moment are good or bad, painful or exciting, sad or happy, depressing or promising, to some degree each of us can still bring some creativity, some courage, some spirit of adventure to this last stage of our lives.
>
> [LeShan, *50 Again*, p. 14]

LeShan comes back to a favorite theme, that we must let go of the past, and combines it with the need to be creative.

> In order to go on using one's most creative human capacities, you have to let go of what has been—be glad for whatever glory there has been in your life, savor every moment, and then look forward to finding new ways of expressing yourself.
>
> [LeShan, *50 Again*, p. 95]

Art Linkletter suggests that this should be easier rather than harder for older people. Although one may think of the elderly as "set in their ways" and inflexible—and indeed many people, both old and young are so—Linkletter believes that the greater experience of older people should increase rather than decrease their ability to change:

> One of the great rewards of growing older is that a person who grows old has experience. . . . By the age of seventy, you learn to handle tough situations and to evaluate them properly. . . . We know a lot more about change than young people do, and this means that we know a lot more about life—because change, after all, is what life is all about.
>
> [Linkletter, *Ageless*, pp. 167-68]

While I was looking about for people who had adapted creatively to their retirement, it occurred to me to look in my own backyard. My husband, who is seventy-seven years old, about a year ago joined a Dixieland jazz band, all but one of whose members are in their upper seventies and using their musical talents to enhance their later years. Three taught at the University of Massachusetts at Amherst, a fourth was the fire chief in Greenfield, and the fifth—my husband and the band's pianist—taught music and band in Virginia and New York schools.

I began to realize what an adaptable group of men were assembled in this jazz band when they came up to our home to rehearse and have lunch one day last year. My husband had just completed building, by himself, a large gazebo behind our house and was eager to show off his handiwork to his friends. It was a lively, laughing gathering, but between the joshing and musical conversation I began to perceive that these men had all entered rewarding post-retirement lives that perhaps built on their earlier work but was not limited to it.

Their band, named the Horse Mountain Jazz Band, meets every Tuesday at the home of Joseph Contino, who worked with the University of Massachusetts Department of Music for thirty-three years in various positions—as director of bands and as a teacher of clarinet, other woodwind instruments, and various advanced music courses. Since his retirement in 1983, he has organized and directed chamber music workshops and also begun to study the viola, an instrument that could not be more different from his clarinet. He has met with sufficient success in this new venture to become a violist in various local groups,

including the Valley Light Opera Company, the Holyoke Civic Orchestra, and various quartets. Occasionally, however, he departs to other states and even to Germany to star as a grandfather par excellence, a role in which he reports that he is not only happy but very successful.

The oldest by a year or so is Paul Lemeris, the band's drummer and business manager. An Army professional, Paul retired from the service in 1962, after which he worked in a Boston bank until he entered the Department of Zoology at the University of Massachusetts. Paul's post-retirement activities could not be guessed from his resume. Not only is he a very good drummer, who continues to take lessons to improve his technique, but he also excels at tennis, still plays singles, and gives lessons in the sport.

Ted Rising, the band's banjo player, also works with a professional teacher to hone his musical skills. A distinguished industrial engineer specializing in the public health field, Ted held many supervisory and teaching positions at the

University of Massachusetts. He also has served as consultant to numerous organizations, written three books in his field, and contributed articles, chapters, and papers to many other publications. Ted, like his colleagues, is athletically active, skiing and canoeing frequently.

The trumpeter, Bill Collings, spent 38 years with the Greenfield Fire Department, retiring as its Chief at the mandatory age in 1987. He also remained as long as allowed in the Air Force Reserve. Meanwhile, he built his own home and worked to help others do so. Having played trumpet since high school, Bill increased the hours spent in this rewarding skill at retirement and now plays in six local community bands and several dance bands.

The sixth member, the trombonist, is the only musician in the band under retirement

Taking time to be Grandfather adds to the quality of life for the Horse Mountain Jazz Band members Joseph Contino, who makes the acquaintance of his day-old granddaughter, Fiora, top, and Ted Rising, who reads a favorite bedtime story to his grandson, Andrew.
—photographs courtesy of Joseph Contino and Ted Rising

age. J. J. Silva is still an active professional musician working out of New York City and the master of many instruments.

Accepting and adapting becomes more difficult for people in their eighties and nineties, as physical and sometimes mental abilities decline. I had the privilege recently of interviewing a couple who provided a wonderful example of the ability to adapt their lives as required by their aging. As you will see from their story, they demonstrate many of the responses to old age that the authors just quoted have been recommending: accepting the need to slow down, exercising control, remaining flexible, and being creative in new ways.

Bob and Annabelle Haven, ninety-one and eighty-seven respectively, live in an apartment in Athol connected to the law office that he founded and in which he practiced law for fifty-five years. They have been married even longer than that— sixty-three years—and that it has been a happy marriage is obvious from their demeanor with each other.

In earlier days, they lived in a Cape Cod colonial house in Orange for which Bob did most of the restoration work. Says Annabelle, "Bob can do anything." They had cats, dogs, goats, and chickens, because they both greatly enjoy animals. She was active in the Petersham Crafts Center, where she learned crewel work and produced some exceptional pieces. She showed me an exquisite four-panel screen that she had designed and made. Originally displayed at the center and then used as drapes in their house, the crewel work is now in a frame that Bob made for it. The Havens had two children leading to their present eight great-grandchildren. Bob and Annabelle were the center of the family, hosting frequent big family dinners. Summers were spent in a "camp" that was built by Bob near a New Hampshire lake.

A lot has changed and nothing has changed. Instead of living in a house with gardens and acreage, they make their home in an in-town apartment where they have extensive flower beds tended with their son's help. Instead of owning and caring for many animals in and around their home, they feed and stroke the neighborhood cats that come to the patio in back. Instead of summering at the New Hampshire camp this year, which is quite a distance from any hospital, they plan to set out feeders in back and lure some birds to watch. Instead of preparing the family dinners, they attend them when they feel able to do so. Instead of suggesting what the younger family members should do, they themselves are now receiving suggestions. So do they feel sorry for themselves? Not at all. I heard only thankfulness for what they have, not regrets for what is past. They both still "get about," and they have each other. What has not changed are the love between them and the love maintained with their family.

Annabelle and Bob Haven of Athol, Massachusetts, discuss garden plans.

—photograph by R. Rand Haven, Jr.

And Annabelle as recently as 1994 blossomed forth as a published author. She explained that she has always done some writing of poems and stories, and that she loved to tell children her favorite stories from her own childhood. But she was fully occupied with her family and that came first, before her own desire to write. Then her son, now practicing law next door, urged her to write down the stories, which became the book engagingly titled, *Listen, My Dears*. Not only are the stories charming and amusing, but they describe what life was like before 1920. Now she has her own corner in the apartment, with a desk and typewriter, while her husband has his special area, and they both "do their own thing" much of the day. And she is continuing to write. As for the crewel work, Annabelle says, with a slight wave of the hand and without apparent sadness, that her eyes are no longer up to it, that it is a thing of the past. She does know, however, that it will be treasured in the future by her descendants, and that gives her pleasure.

The Havens are an example of a couple who "did it right," first with their marriage and then with their adaptations to the restrictions of old age. In fact, just about every one of the people past eighty whom I interviewed have begun adapting with little fuss. Each time in the pages ahead that you meet one of these successful elders, you will note that they have not hardheadedly refused to adapt nor have they mourned the necessity. They have simply said, "O.K., I guess this is necessary. I'll do it." And they have done it.

One of the hardest adaptations occurs between the generations, when the children—themselves usually in their sixties—"take over" their parents. As the parents begin to show signs of confusion and memory loss, their children feel that, to keep finances straight, they must handle the checkbook and any investments. Surrender of the checkbook always hurts the spirit of elderly persons, whose independence has become closely connected with their ability to handle their own affairs. "I did it well all these years, why not now? Do you think I am senile?" I have been told that the cruel answer given by one or two of the already "young old" children has been, "Yes, you are."

About the same time, the children want to schedule and attend their parents' medical appointments, to make sure that they are getting the best of care and understand what medications they should take and when. This part of the takeover is generally more readily accepted.

Then there is the question of living arrangements. Can Mom or Dad live alone safely? And if the answer is no, not with complete safety, then who decides when and to what kind of facility the parent should move? Usually, the parent prefers to continue to live at home, and often this is possible with home care arrangements like those in Franklin County, Massachusetts, where household help, nursing care, and daily meals can be provided. The predilection of the adult children is often to get Mom and Dad to a place where they will be completely cared for, so that there will be no more worrying about them. And, of course, complete care means the much-feared nursing home. Sometimes, one of the children will open her own home to the parent, who then may become like a child in her own child's home. Not easy either.

I am saddened every time I witness the takeover occurring, and instinctively I ready myself for a fight on behalf of my friend. Perhaps I view the situation too subjectively, envisioning one of my children telling me what to do if I become physically dependent and mentally less acute. To my surprise, most of the old parents give in rather easily to being controlled by their children, at first complaining quite bitterly to me but finally accepting the situation. Most are willing to surrender their independence, often before that becomes absolutely necessary, in exchange for their children's continued affection and approval and for whatever physical assistance has become necessary.

Observing the phenomenon of takeover and eventual acceptance a number of times, I have concluded that the role reversal is more palatable when initiated by the parent. After all, it is easier to hand over control than to have it wrested from one. A smart parent will try to perceive when financial, medical, or residential independence is no longer possible, while a considerate adult child will attempt to let the parent make the decisions leading to dependence.

Adapting is particularly necessary for the "old old," but even those of us who are in early old age, who have only recently retired, are in a similar position. We also must adapt, change, and choose to move forward. We are in the position of making what may be difficult and far-reaching decisions. Arthur Schlesinger, Jr., professor and historian, puts the problem concisely.

> In your seventies, time becomes the most precious of commodities. The thing I resent most is wasting it. Up until the age of seventy time seems infinite, but time is now finite.
>
> [Schlesinger, *Ageless*, p. 241]

Perhaps the most important choice is how we will use the active time we have left.

Coping with Loneliness, Boredom, and Depression

Ironically, the time left, so very precious and sometimes seeming to fly by us, often also seems too long, even heavy, for many very elderly people. The problem for these persons is what to do with it.

Lurking in the background for the "young old" and often prominent in the foreground for the "old old," are the big three—loneliness, boredom, and depression—intertwined. My observations and reading all point to four major ways to both cope with these and also use the precious remaining time in a fulfilling manner.

Interacting with People

On the face of it, to suggest interaction with people as an antidote for loneliness sounds foolish. A lonely person would say, "If I had interaction with people, of course I would not be lonely." Which is not necessarily so, as my experience with Harriet, described later, suggests. The isolation of many elders changes their situation vis-à-vis other people. Previously, other people were a natural part of their lives, in their marriages and employment. When they needed companionship, they could drive somewhere to find it. Now, however, often widowed, retired, and no longer driving, they find themselves alone. The only companionship for many of the "old old" comes from social workers and volunteer staff.

*Mildred Crossman of
Bernardston, Massachusetts,
welcomes a visitor with her
million-dollar smile.*

At this stage in life, if one lives alone and cannot go out to find people, inter-action with others usually requires constant effort. It does not come naturally as it did before, and there will likely be less of it. The problem, therefore, is how to live alone without being lonely. Or, more realistically, how to be less lonely less often.

I have observed several partial solutions. Mildred Crossman comes to mind as an example of someone who, although in the classic position of one who might be lonely, bored, and depressed—living alone, very old, walking with difficulty, no nearby relatives—has done an excellent job of handling her situation. Mildred is ninety-eight years old, mentally alert but with a major hearing loss. She has lived alone since her parents' deaths about twenty years ago. Although she has had the services for a number of years of the home care agency for which I volunteer, I was called to visit her only after the death of her son and then more as someone to help her handle this crisis in her life. I assume that she had not complained of loneliness earlier, or her case worker would have assigned a com-panion to her earlier.

The first thing I noticed about Mildred was that she smiled not only on greet-ing me but much of the time I was with her. She has a lovely smile, about which she is often complimented and on which she rightly prides herself. This smile has increased my pleasure in visiting her and is undoubtedly one of the reasons

Suggestions To Alleviate Loneliness

Make yourself pleasant to be with. Try to make smiling a habit, and in particular avoid having a "long face," which is all too common in the "old old." I would add to this that one should also at least seem interested in the other person, by always looking at the speaker and often expressing interest in the other person's life.

Work at finding and keeping friends. Make the effort to correspond with and telephone to old friends, and be open to making new ones, particularly with people younger than you, who tend to live longer. Try to maintain interest in what new friends are doing. As long as you can, attend social events where you may meet new people and acquire additional interests. And even make conversation with people whose contact with you is not primarily social. Most older people instinctively do this, sometimes too much.

Accept help from other people. It is a much forgotten axiom that we tend to like those we help more than those who help us. Learning to accept a certain amount of dependence is not easy, but it does attract other people to you and increases their concern for you.

If you enjoy animals, acquire a pet. A cat or dog is best, because they usually like physical contact and require frequent attention, but even a bird is some company. Most older people, even those who find walking difficult, are able to provide the minimal care required by a dog and particularly by a cat, which does not even need to be let outside. And with the advent of clumpable kitty litter, it is not necessary to empty all the contents of a cat box.

Let in the outside world. Through reading, radio, or television, the outside world is readily available. In the first, other people are talking to you through your eyes and your imagination. In the second, they are speaking to you through your ears and imagination. In the third, both eyes and ears bring them into your home. Few older people are both completely blind and entirely deaf, so almost everyone can get access to outside experiences and other people through one of these media. The three media are a wonderful way for older people to leave their worrisome world of cares and pains behind as they enter a different world, however briefly. And for tomorrow's elders, there will also be the Internet.

other people continue to come see her. She is a pleasant and cheerful person to be with.

My next observation, upheld through later visits, was that she is very involved with and interested in about fifteen people in addition to her relatives: her late son's wife, four or five local friends, several old friends who have moved away (but with whom she corresponds), and the people who provide her daily or weekly services, including the mail deliverer and all of us sent out from the home care agency, who supply meals, cleaning, personal care, and companionship. While she was able to do so, Mildred attended the local senior center's lunches. And she still daily telephones to an old friend who, despite being in an advanced stage of Alzheimer's disease, answers the phone and knows Mildred. It is clear that Mildred is not only interested in other people but also willing to make some effort to remain in touch with many of them.

Mildred's third defense against loneliness is owning a pet. The importance of a pet became very clear indeed when her thirteen-year-old dog died about a year ago. She was devastated, quite overwhelmed with grief. Not only was she lonely without this little dog to care for and talk to, but she was fearful when she heard noises in her house at night.

In her typical fashion, Mildred let all her friends know about her loss, and many of us were inspired to try very hard to find her another dog of the kind she wanted. Eventually such a dog was found, and Mildred is again much more contented. Even though she sometimes finds it difficult to care for Pixie, she knows how important the dog is to her happiness and is not shy about letting those who come to her house help her put Pixie out on her leash. Which further ties people to her.

As do many homebound elders, Mildred watches television, primarily soap operas. When I arrive at her home, I can tell that she finds it hard to turn off her

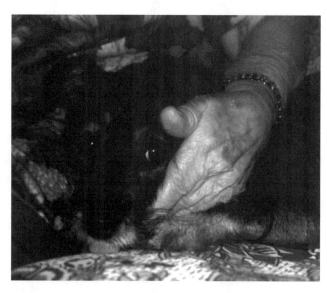

Mildred Crossman's dog Pixie luxuriates in her mistress's love and, incidentally, provides Mildred with companionship and one of many reasons to be interested in each day.

stories. She would really like to watch the television during our visit, as she has sometimes, turning off the sound and just stealing glances at the closed-captioned words. Although I have tended to scorn soap operas, I have learned that Mildred's interest in the characters takes her out of herself during the long afternoons and provides some "company" for her.

Mildred is a living example of the efficacy of five specific ways of alleviating or even preventing loneliness for the "old old," but they are also applicable to those of us who are younger, because acquiring good habits takes a while. My experience with Mildred, repeated to various degrees with other elderly people, has led to the suggestions on the previous page.

We can more readily apply the five techniques to ourselves than suggest them to others, except indirectly. I cannot—and do not—come into the home of someone who has complained of loneliness, assess her situation with my five methods in mind, and then baldly suggest that she be more pleasant, for example.

Only occasionally does someone really pick up on a specific suggestion directly put. Indirect suggestions have been more often effective. Ultimately, my most valuable contribution to a lonely person has been simply time and commitment to careful listening. Through my weekly visit I provide at least one or two hours of pleasant companionship and offer an opportunity for her to talk non-stop if she wishes. I also try to leave a thought or two behind about the outside world. In return, I myself take away a thought or two about how I may better prepare for my own old age.

Maintaining or initiating involvement with other people is a major theme of the literature on successful aging. Usually the advice is given to the "young old," to those who still have wider choices than the elders I visit. Betty Friedan, herself always politically and socially active, recommends community involvement for elders in her book, *Fountain of Age.*

> Some studies indicate that the sheer number of ties with the community predicts a vital, long life. This doesn't mean empty, stay-busy activities—but valid purposes and projects in the community.
>
> [Friedan, *Parade Magazine*, p. 6]

Dr. Hallowell agrees, saying succinctly,

> The key to successful aging is *involvement.*
>
> [Hallowell, p. 26]

He later points more specifically to friends and acquaintances, backing up his statement with research:

> Studies have found that those whose minds have remained lively and clear tend to share certain characteristics. One of them is that they have numerous friends or acquain-

tances with whom they are in frequent communication. . . . [E]lderly people who live in families actually increase their mental abilities over a number of years, whereas those who live alone or who have withdrawn from society lose, to some degree, their ability to think.

[Hallowell, pp. 55-56]

George Leonard, author and athlete, made the following astute observation about older people who become self-absorbed:

I've had a chance to look at aging in America because my mother lives in a retirement community. I see that people who didn't have many resources, who were not very interested in life when they were younger, become miserable rather quickly. I've noticed that as you get older you desperately need other people, friends and so forth. If you're preoccupied with yourself, you've had it—the whole universe will become yourself. The universe will become your pains and aches and your complaints, and when the universe becomes your complaint, then it's not a very nice place to live in.

[Leonard, *Ageless*, pp. 148-49]

How often I have seen it happen. The most absorbing and often exclusive topic in the world for many of the "old old" is their health. Some of my friends can spend the better part of two hours telling and retelling me about their physical problems, visits to the doctor, suggestions by the pharmacists, and medical bills.

Cowley, like Leonard, believes that early involvement with others carries rewards into later life:

At a time when so much depends on the past, those who have led rich lives are rewarded by having richer memories. Those who have loved are more likely to be loved in return. In spite of accidents and ingratitude, those who have served others are a little more likely to be served. The selfish and heartless will suffer most from the heartlessness of others, if they live long enough; they have their punishment on earth.

[Cowley, p. 55]

Cowley's opinion on how early characteristics affect the quality of a person's old age is hardly new. Plato, quoting "aged Cephalus" speaking to Socrates in *The Republic*, writes:

"It is not old age but men's characters and temperaments; for the man who has a calm and happy disposition will scarcely feel the pressure of age. The man who is of the opposite disposition finds that both youth and old age are equally troublesome."

[Plato, *Oxford*, p. 230]

The importance of maintaining and nurturing our friendships is not unexpectedly attested to by LeShan:

We must also tend to our relationships with others as well as garnering time to be alone; love is the most healing of all powers at our disposal—we need to have it and give it even more than we need a balanced diet.

[LeShan, *50 Again*, p. 141]

Sarton, who spent many hours corresponding with friends around the world, treasured them as essential, particularly during periods of difficulty:

Speaking of friends, certainly they are enormously important. Without them, I probably would have suffered some kind of breakdown.

[Sarton, *Endgame*, p. 65]

Scott-Maxwell, after saying how hard she tries to conceal the extent of her pain and loneliness, points out that older friends are more likely to understand:

I wonder if we need be quite so dutiful. With one friend of my own age we cheerfully exchange the worst symptoms, and our black dreads as well. We frequently talk of death, for we are very alert to the experience of the unknown that may be so near and it is only to those of one's own age that one can speak frankly.

[Scott-Maxwell, p. 31]

Bella Lewitzky, dancer, choreographer, and teacher, comments at seventy-five on her increasing acceptance of other people.

It's funny, but as I've aged I've grown more confident in my own values yet, at the same time, more tolerant of differences.

[Lewitsky, *Ageless*, p. 161]

This acceptance and ability to understand, this empathy, is often a talent of the elderly, who have experienced so many emotions that they may be more sensitive to, more able to feel into, the situation of others.

Before empathy, there must be interest. Very few of the elderly people I visit as a weekly companion or counselor have any real interest in knowing who I am, why I want to visit them, or anything except passing details of my everyday life. One or two may ask initially where I came from and why my husband and I moved from Washington, D.C., to Warwick, Massachusetts. But nothing beyond that. As I look over the list of the many people I have visited in connection with programs for the elderly, I realize that the interest of all but two is almost exclusively in themselves, their aches and pains, the minor events of their own lives, and sometimes in their relatives and old friends.

One of the two people who really wanted to know something about me was Elaine, the gracious lady who never talked about her own illness. She in fact would push me at times to tell more about what I was doing and why. The other person is Jane, a delightful lady to be discussed later, who tells stories at great length about all branches of her family. She is able to pause long enough in her efforts to inquire about and even listen to what is going on in my life. Upon occasion, I have asked for her advice, which has been good.

You will remember that I primarily visit elderly people who are admittedly lonely, depressed, or bored. Although I do not know what their personalities were like when they were young, I suspect that if they had broken out of their self-concern and felt more sincere interest in other people during their earlier years, they might have avoided at least some of the distress they now experience.

An outstanding example of someone in her late eighties who has maintained her interaction with other people and who experiences none of the three problems is Barbara Ellis, the "artist with a passion" described earlier. So accustomed have I become to self-absorption by the elderly in need of my visits, that I admit to being quite surprised during my interview with her by the interest she showed in me as a person. Not just what was I writing, why did I move to Massachusetts, and what did I want to know for my book. Mid-interview, she turned to me forthrightly and said, "Now, I want to ask you a few questions."And she did, with the result that I think I told her as much or more about myself than she told me about herself and her view of aging. I felt not only her interest but her empathy for what I was telling her about my life. No wonder she has many friends of all ages.

Perhaps Barbara was always able to elicit such free responses from others, as I am certain she has always enjoyed other people. It is also likely that her abilities have developed over time. Empathy and sensitivity to others seem become well-developed only after one lives awhile.

Scott-Maxwell exhibits this sensitivity and an exquisite perception in her discussions of her relationship with other people:

> When I am with other people I try to find them, or try to find a point in myself from which to make a bridge to them, or I walk on the egg-shells of affection trying not to hurt or misjudge. All this is very tiring, but love at any age takes everything you've got.
>
> [Scott-Maxwell, pp. 14-15]

She explains the difficulty of sustaining open and loving relationships when one is old and in pain. She recommends the always difficult middle road:

> One cannot be honest even at the end of one's life, for no one is wholly alone. We are bound to those we love, or to those who love us, and to those who need us to be brave, or content, or even happy enough to allow them not to worry about us. So we must refrain from giving pain, as our last gift to our fellows. For love of humanity consume as much of your travail as you can. Not all, never that terrible muteness that drains away human warmth. But when we are almost free of life we must retain guile that those still caught in life may not suffer more. The old must often try to be silent, if it is within their power, since silence may be like space, the intensely alive something that contains all. The clear echo of what we refrained from saying, everything, from the first pause of understanding, to the quiet of comprehension.
>
> [Scott-Maxwell, pp. 142-43]

Harton notes in a very realistic manner how the old may be able to affect the younger in a beneficial way:

These characteristics which can flower so genially and graciously with age may produce a certain very precious gift, namely, the power to bring out the best in people and to enlarge their normal capacities for goodness. . . . It is true that sometimes the very old have not sufficient force to give much active sympathy or concentrated attention but the accepted discipline of years of duty, suffering and perseverance in following the light, has refined the soul into a glowing ember of patient charity and this in itself warms and elevates those who draw near.

[Harton, p. 123]

Interaction with acquaintances, friends, and family is helpful, but intimacy with someone is even better. Betty Friedan carefully defines and describes this intimacy, which may or may not be sexual.

For the process of "disclosing oneself to another" is the essence of intimacy. It may be experienced or enhanced by physical touching, but the touching of the human heart is through words.

[Friedan, *Fountain*, p. 266]

She says that research shows that

ties of intimacy are the most important guarantee of a vital, long life. This implies, for both women and men, moving beyond the sexual measures of youth. . . .

We don't have to love or be loved the way we loved when we were 17 or 30, or not love at all. It isn't an either/or. There are new ways to love.

[Friedan, *Parade Magazine*, p. 5]

She believes the following choice is possible.

Woman or man, we begin to know, before it is too late, that we can *choose* to tear down the walls we have built up against that joyous, painful intimacy, *choose* to take the risks of it, *choose* to create the experiences, reunions, that will keep it alive, over the distances of time and space.

[Friedan, *Fountain*, p. 299]

For the unmarried—whether divorced, widowed, or never married—a special person with whom to be intimate is not always on the scene. Wondering how such a situation might be handled successfully, I asked a fellow elder peer counselor, a smiling and very bright single lady just on the eighty-year-old line. Grace Blanchard was born in Greenfield, spent many years in Waltham, Massachusetts, and then returned to Greenfield after she retired. Educated as a teacher, she soon discovered her true calling as a physician's assistant and spent many happy years in that profession.

During her time in Waltham, she shared living quarters with a classmate from college years and over time they became fast friends, regularly attending Boston Symphony concerts together. They had an arrangement, however, that each would go her own way and make her own friends, which they did. Grace, who had

Grace Blanchard of Greenfield, Massachusetts, studies a book about Alzheimer's disease to help her counsel a new client.

attended the Methodist church in Greenfield, became active in a Methodist church close to Harvard Square. She became one of the valued resident members in what was basically a church for college students.

As Grace told me about her life, I realized that she has a talent for helping people on a one-to-one basis. Her medical activities obviously used her talent for inspiring confidence in people. Her years of working as an elder peer counselor gave her additional experience in this type of relationship. When she returned in her mid-sixties to Greenfield, she became active again in the Methodist church there. She also began serving as a "hostess" in the Church Street Home, which is a retirement home for about eight elderly women. As a hostess, Grace would be on duty, day and night for three days, to oversee everything that occurred in the home, making sure that appropriate meals were served, providing whatever help might be needed for each guest, and presiding over the dinner table. What struck me was Grace's firm remark that whenever she served as hostess, she made it a point to have some time alone with each resident, so that each one would know that she cared about her. Needless to say, she has always been very popular at the Church Street Home. And she still returns occasionally, although only as a substitute.

A multitude of one-to-one relationships is still not intimacy, but it goes a long way toward it. Grace's caring for people, for who they really are and what they need, has made her many close friends. She still retains her longtime friendship with her Waltham roommate, despite the friend's dementia that has changed its nature. She even took her annual week-long vacation with this friend, adapting to the situation by using her own home as a base for day-trips during the week. When I asked Grace if she herself still derives something positive from this friendship, she quickly responded yes. And I gathered from other parts of our conversation that this was not her only close relationship over the years.

While intimacy is perhaps more available for the married, certainly marriage does not always bring with it the spiritual intimacy that makes it valuable. Or often the intimacy has disappeared with time. The Havens, whose ability to adapt to aging was described a few pages earlier, are indeed living a vital, long life, which they attribute to their marriage. I cannot resist sketching a moment during my interview with them. I was sitting close to and facing them both when I asked a blunt question: "In one or two words, to what would you attribute your successful old age?" Immediately, I added, "I think I know what you are going to say." But I didn't, not exactly. They looked at each other with very moving love in their eyes, holding each other's gaze, and then she turned to me and said, "Being together." I had expected them to say, simply, "Love." But this was better. It was more personal, each to the other.

Intimacy does not rule out a desire for occasional solitude. Despite the authors' clear agreement on the necessity of keeping friendship, love, and intimacy within our lives, there occurs now and then with some of them a longing for solitude, more perhaps than with younger people. The need for solitude runs throughout Sarton's journals, as well as in the writings of Scott-Maxwell, who is quoted below.

> Without loving letters, and with no friendly voice on the 'phone, lacking the loyal concern of one's family? May I never have that to face, but still—the basic need for me is to meet alone and in silence all that puzzles and pains me and to wait until the turmoil is stilled.
>
> [Scott-Maxwell, p. 46]

> Only this morning—this mild, sunny morning that charmed me into happiness—I realize my cheer was partly because I was alone.
>
> [Scott-Maxwell, p. 65]

Time alone may be well spent in various ways: pursuing a new creative goal, performing daily tasks, enjoying one of the solitary pleasures that are shared by young and old alike, remembering and musing about one's past life, or perhaps even attaining spiritual depths previously unavailable. All are discussed in the following pages.

Working with Purpose

Involvement with people is not enough to counteract loneliness, much less boredom. Harriet is a prime illustration. She is a charming widow in her mid-eighties. Although she is far from being as physically fit as the historian Charlotte Ryan, she still drives a car and walks without a cane. She lives with her beloved little cat in her own house in a middle-income neighborhood. Every week Harriet attends a crafts class and regularly goes to church and its women's group. She often volunteers to help in the church's fairs and suppers. Her son and daughter-in-law telephone and visit often. Occasionally, she visits grandchildren or friends for a week at a time in other cities. She watches television quiz programs, mainly in the evenings. She knows that, in comparison to many people of her age, she is very fortunate.

Despite all her contact with other people, Harriet's urgent complaint is loneliness, which she feels has caused the depression she experiences, particularly in the mornings. I have gradually discovered, however, that Harriet has many, many friends and acquaintances with whom she talks by phone and often plans lunches or expeditions of one sort of another. Nevertheless, she feels she has few friends and, while expressing her thankfulness for her health and other good fortune, she refers frequently to her loneliness.

Harriet's situation fascinates me, because she seems to be doing everything right to counteract loneliness. Yet I sense that she is merely trying to pass the time as pleasantly as possible until she dies. Probably she has some chemical imbalance that is at least a partial cause of her morning depression, because medication has seemed to help slightly. But I gradually began to suspect that there was a psychological reason as well. As I regularly listened to her recital of what she had been doing during the past week, I became aware that she lacked perhaps the most important antidote to boredom—a purpose in life, a reason to want to get up in the morning. Surviving another day and visiting with friends and family is not sufficient for her at this time of her life.

The importance of a purpose cannot be overstated. Harriet lost her single purpose when her husband died. Providing a home and companionship for him and then nursing him through his final illness had been her purpose. He died, and she lost a reason for living. Replacing a purpose in one's eighties is no easy matter. It certainly is unlikely to be supplied by a counselor like me.

Nevertheless, I searched my mind for possible purposes for Harriet. I ran through a list of my clients, past and present, to find out what their purposes were—if they had any, which was rare. I found two whose purpose seemed to be to make each day easier and more pleasant for the person with whom they lived, a son in each case. But what about those living alone, which is more usual? Of these, two had a purpose of sorts that seemed to partially assuage their boredom but would certainly be quite insufficient for Harriet. Each one was trying to knit or crochet enough doilies or socks to give as presents. They felt a certain pressure to get the work done. A side benefit was that they enjoyed their reading or watching television more because they felt they really should be knitting or crocheting. Both these women are unable to leave home unaided.

Back to Harriet. Because she still is able to drive, I suggested that, like me, she visit the elderly. I thought this would also solve the "lonely" problem. Her response was that she finds older people "depressing." I tried to dissuade her from this notion by telling her, from my own experience, that the truth is exactly the opposite. My spirits usually get quite a lift from the visits. They provide me with some of the contact with people that I myself need and enjoy, and I get the boost that comes with knowing that I have been useful to someone. With Harriet, it came down to not wanting to do anything that she felt would not be immediately and obviously pleasurable. A self-defeating attitude. I was left with encouraging her in the several "good deeds" that she already performs for aging acquaintances.

One cannot help comparing Harriet with Barbara Ellis and Charlotte Ryan, also widows, whose driving purposes—to paint and to write, respectively—help guard them against loneliness, boredom, and depression.

Still another comparison came to mind. I interviewed a woman who, like Harriet, is gregarious by nature and still drives a car. Arline Cohn at eighty is a few years younger than Harriet and is not a widow, which of course makes her less likely to be lonely. But there is another difference equally important.

Arline, unlike Harriet, finds the frequent interaction with people that she needs and enjoys through helping individuals and working for causes that interest her. She receives pleasure as a by-product, but it is not her aim, as it is for Harriet.

Arline Cohn of Greenfield, Massachusetts, contacts volunteers for one of her projects.

Arline knows that she is fortunate to be gregarious and optimistic by nature. To me, it is what she has done with these characteristics that is important. After coming to Greenfield with her husband and family, she spent most of her time on volunteer activities. Almost any activity in Greenfield that one can name has probably had Arline on its board of directors. Among her major interests are the Greenfield Community College, the Society for the Prevention of Cruelty to Children, the Franklin Medical Center, and the elder peer counseling program. When she is not working for a good cause, she might be attending a book club, playing bridge, attending cultural events, or visiting a museum. All this during the daytime. At night there are books and knitting.

At eighty, she has not yet slowed down very much. She notices that she tires a bit more easily and has accordingly pulled back a little from some of her activities. Her husband has health problems, which makes them both aware of their age. She says they are just thankful for the wonderful lives they have had so far and for their loving children and grandchildren. They try to enjoy each day. Arline laughingly quoted a little saying that she says she often thinks of: "Yesterday is past; tomorrow is not here; and today is a gift. That is why it is called the 'present.'"

When I asked Arline what she believes is the key to successful aging, she agreed with everyone else whom I have asked—namely, health. The second key she identified as "having many interests." You will note that she did not say "friends," but "interests." Arline is not a person with a single purpose, but with a multitude of interests, many of them altruistic. In this she resembles Grace, the other elder peer counselor described above, whose interest in music, current affairs, and books made her remark briskly to me, "I can't understand how any intelligent person can ever be bored. There are so many interesting things in the world."

But there are of course many people who have not through the years acquired enough interests or a sufficient purpose in life to ward off boredom. Once they hit their late seventies or eighties, the number of reasons for living that are available to them may be few. For anyone, activities that are useful or aid other people are best. The problem is that a loss of eyesight, hearing, or mobility limits the choices. Some of the very elderly can and do keep in touch with or check on other old people by telephone, making their lives a little larger. Usually woodworking or some kind of handiwork, learned in earlier years, can fill the time. But even such occupations, the only possibilities sometimes remaining, can be curtailed by arthritis, if not by poor eyesight. Need I say that I have recently learned to crochet?

However, for those of us not yet among the "old old," some preparation for later years is still possible. If we have had a career or job outside the home, the

At ninety-eight, Mildred Crossman crochets another doily for a friend.

moment of retirement is crucial. Assuming reasonably good health, retirement these days comes when we still have plenty of energy left. Before retirement, time is at a premium. After settling into retirement, there may well seem to be too much of it. While some people may enjoy flitting from one amusement to the next, most feel the need for purpose at least by the end of a year. We want to feel useful, which requires some sort of "work." And work helps to keep all three problems at bay, but particularly boredom. Just about all authors sing the praises of purposeful, creative work for the elderly. The best songs on the subject follow.

Phillip Berman, in his introduction to a collection of reflections on "our later years," appropriately titled *The Ageless Spirit*, puts well the conflicting desires we face at retirement.

> Time, and how best to use it, presents the active and productive senior with a pleasant yet somewhat vexing paradox. On the one hand, he has a strong need—in some a lifesaving compulsion—to devote himself to creative and meaningful work. On the other hand, after successfully navigating six or more decades he is now wise enough to recognize the importance of savoring life's simple pleasures in a state of enlightened equanimity.
>
> [Berman, *Ageless*, p. 6]

Dr. Hallowell reminds us that we may live a long time after retirement and that we will need more than recreational activities.

> It is wise to keep in mind that the state of being retired can potentially occupy a quarter of a century or a quarter of a lifetime, and that is a lot of time to be bored and depressed. . . .
>
> The most difficult part of retirement is the time. . . . You cannot . . . constantly pursue those leisure activities that were formerly squeezed into weekends and two-week vacations.
>
> [Hallowell, pp. 240-41]

LeShan notes that most people in their sixties still want to work.

Despite the fact that there is very real discrimination against older workers, 25 percent of retirees do continue to seek full- or part-time employment.

A 1981 Harris poll indicated that 75 percent of people under the age of sixty-five want to keep working when they retire. Despite the fact that there is very real discrimination against older workers, 25 percent of retirees do continue to seek full- or part-time employment.

[LeShan, *50 Again,* p. 97]

Dr. Hallowell writes of the emptiness that may be encountered after retirement, basing his statements on the 1981 Harris poll.

Those who were earning the highest salaries looked forward to it the most and were the happiest afterward. Yet longings for the workplace remain very much alive. Most of those polled miss the money, the people they encountered while on the job and the work itself. They also miss the feeling of being useful, the excitement of the activity around them, the respect they received from others and the routine of a fixed schedule.

[Hallowell, p. 236]

The same poll revealed how few people had made some preparation for how they would spend their time.

Only 53 percent of those people sixty-five and over developed hobbies or other activities in preparation for retirement. Only eight percent took a course in retirement preparation; and only 64 percent had built up their savings over the years specifically for retirement.

[Hallowell, pp. 240-41]

Malcolm Boyd, an Episcopal priest and author, in his daily meditations on growing older, emphasizes the need to prepare for how we will spend our post-retirement years. He writes,

It is enormously problematic that we do not build enough relaxation, alternative creativity, or pleasure into our work lives. There is too little time for figuring out what it means to be human. Our collective nose is too close to the grindstone. . . . Suddenly, we seem to have turned over our life to some force that is powerful and alien.

So, it's important to build some aspects of "retirement" into our work life, elements of "work life" into our retirement.

[Boyd, *Rich with Years,* July 15]

Maggie Kuhn, an activist for the organization for older people called The Gray Panthers, points out the necessity of a goal toward which to strive in one's work:

I believe that there has to be a purpose and a goal to life. The secret of thriving and surviving is having a goal. Having a goal is absolutely essential, because it gives you the energy and the drive to do what you must do, and to get up when you feel like staying in bed.

[Kuhn, *Ageless,* p. 129]

Rollo May, therapist and author, believes that the appropriate work for each person is a very individual choice, but it should be inspiring to that person:

I really think creativity is the answer to aging, and by creativity I mean listening to one's own inner voice, to one's own ideas, to one's own aspirations. It may be social work. It may be gardening. It may be building. But it must be something fresh, something new, some idea that takes fire—this is what I'd like to see among older people.

[May, *Ageless*, p. 188]

Obviously, not just any work will suffice. B. F. Skinner at seventy-nine gives this advice.

You must get more out of what you do than an escape from feeling guilty because you are idle. Instead of trying hard to enjoy what you are doing, try hard to find something that you like better.

[Skinner, p. 84]

Cowley at eighty describes the kind of work that is necessary to the spirit:

Poet or housewife, businessman or teacher, every old person needs a work project if he wants to keep himself more alive.

It should be big enough to demand his best efforts, yet not so big as to dishearten him and let him fall back into apathy.

[Cowley, p. 67]

Bernard Berenson at eighty-nine is positively enthusiastic about the pleasure of his work:

1954—a year in which Old Age has increasingly got hold of me, making me timid about going downstairs, increasing every natural deficiency, restricting more and more the time I can walk, or talk, or work. On the other hand, I have never enjoyed work more than now. Indeed, it is almost the "only carnal pleasure" left me.

[Berenson, *Songs*, p. 122]

And anyone reading Sarton's journals realizes how crucial to her psychological well-being was her physical and mental ability to write. Her increasing fame and many friends were no substitute for her work. Late in her seventies, after the shock of being told that she would never be well again, she turned for solace and purpose to her work:

The worst part of the struggle has been that sometimes there seems to be no reason for getting up. But now that I do write a little in the journal, I have, as it were, put on my work clothes again, am a functioning person for a change. It is forcing a change in me toward life. High time.

[Sarton, *Endgame*, p. 22]

And what about the very old and frail? Even for some nursing home residents, writing may be a possibility. *The Atlantic Monthly* article about the nursing home resident who was in love was primarily the story of a writing club there which inspired the former English teacher to write her life story. It has the ring of real life.

I had wondered if I might suffer initially from writer's block, but nothing of that sort occurred. In fact I was flooded by memories—overwhelmed, engulfed, as I sat in my chair by the picture window, writing on my lap board. I was not even aware of the world outside, my head was so full of the people and places of the past, rising up in my mind as they were then, in all the fullness of life, and myself as I was then, that headstrong girl longing to leave her home in east Virginia and walk in the world at large.

I wrote and wrote. I wrote for three days. I wrote until I felt satisfied, and then I stopped. I felt better than I had in years, full of new life and freedom (a paradox, since I am more and more confined to this chair).

[Smith, *The Atlantic Monthly*, p. 111]

Dr. Bortz implies that work may in fact be a type of cure-all, quoting Sir William Osler as saying very simply that

"work is the master therapy."

[Bortz, p. 100]

LeShan says much the same thing, emphasizing the need still to feel useful.

The search for meaning, for seeing our lives as useful and purposeful—feeling that the world would be a poorer place without us—is a fundamental necessity all through life, but never more significant than when we begin to get old.

[LeShan, *50 Again,* p. 93]

Perhaps the past may sometimes at least partially make up for the present, so that people will feel that they indeed have "made a difference." Vining notes a wise remark by an aging friend that may be comforting to some.

Helen yesterday said something rather interesting about aging. . . . It was something about recognizing and accepting that one is no longer useful to . . . anyone, but taking strength from the fact that one has been useful in the past.

[Vining, p. 25]

Establishing a Routine

An important adjunct to purposeful work is routine. B. F. Skinner gives this practical advice.

With a good routine you will not need to make decisions about what is to be done and when, and you will not so often put off enjoyable activities until it is too late.

[Skinner, p. 98]

Writing before the age of seventy, May Sarton spoke eloquently of the value of routine in her life:

How supportive a routine is, how the spirit moves around freely in it as it does in a plain New England church. Routine is not a prison, but the way into freedom from time. The apparently measured time has immeasurable space within it, and in this it resembles music.

[Sarton, Plant, pp. 56-57]

A routine became perhaps even more important to Sarton when in her late seventies she became too ill to write. Again and again she relied on her routine and her work when possible to lift her spirits. She wrote the following in her seventy-ninth and eightieth years:

> I am proud of the fact that I keep to such discipline as it took, for instance today with bad cramps, to get up and get my breakfast, carry it up on the tray, have it in bed, and then get up and make my bed, and finally decide what to wear. . . . As I have said before, the routine is what keeps me from going to pieces.

[Sarton, Encore, pp. 141-42]

The contribution of organization toward longevity was an important finding in a recent study, reported by Betty Friedan:

> The strongest predictor for survival in the twenty-five-year National Institute of Mental Health Longitudinal Study—better than any other factor, except smoking, to indicate who would survive until eighty-one—was "highly organized behavior." . . . the degree of organization and complexity of a person's daily behavior.

[Friedan, Fountain, p. 81]

Friedan herself advised:

> Purposes and projects that structure your days are the most important guarantee of a long and vital life. The ability to find new ones, therefore, and to build and renew skills has to be cultivated now.

[Friedan, Parade Magazine, p. 5]

I came upon another testimony to routine and purpose in a March 2, 1998, Newsweek article by Argus J. Tresidder, a man in his nineties. In his one-page article, "Longevity and Livability," he describes the routine in his "orderly, busy life," which includes walking with an escort, writing novels and stories, listening to audio books, and visiting friends. He has had the sense to request and accept help from neighbors and employees, which in turn has brought him more friends. The theme of his article is that the old deserve respect. Its picture of how he has managed his old age will inspire many people to follow his example.

I met another living example—or rather, two living examples, because they are married to each other—of the value of a structured life. I am referring to Burt and Alice Newton of Athol. When I alerted them that toward the middle of the interview I would ask them to identify the most important factor in their happiness in their mid-eighties, without waiting for the question both Alice and Burt immediately responded, "Routine." And we all laughed, because my husband and I both also find a scheduled way of life relaxing and pleasurable.

Burt and Alice Newton of Athol, Massachusetts, enjoy a breakfast interchange.

Then Alice started to tell the story of their morning routine, saying that Burt gets up at six, while she rises at seven, and that he makes the breakfast. At this point, Burt couldn't resist continuing the story, explaining that he first gets the newspaper and then starts the coffee. Alice smiled, knowing what he would say next. He continued as expected, saying that if the newspaper hasn't come, he forgets to start the coffee and doesn't start it until the paper does arrive. He explained that he has this routine and loves to stick with it. Alice agreed, and laughingly remarked that the routine continues even at breakfast, when they always say the same things to each other. I interjected that with my husband and me that would be, "How did you sleep last night?" and "What are your plans for the day?" The Newtons nodded. Later they said that the structuring of their days to their mutual satisfaction developed after his retirement and took a bit of thought.

Part of the routine involves each having their own place of work. Burt has an active framing shop in the basement, and considers his constant activity there merely a hobby. Alice, retired from her position as director of the Athol library, spends most of her time in a small sun room, where she keeps up with current events, completes crossword puzzles, and writes many long letters to children and lifelong friends. She also is writing memoirs of her childhood and making pictorial genealogies from old family photographs for their children and grandchildren. In addition, she is the primary cook of the family, while he is the gardener.

Like the other happy elders I interviewed, the Newtons are not only busy but attentive to the outside world. Family is big with them, but they seem not to be dependent on it. Alice remarked that just about everything in their living room was "by, of, or from" one of their three children or their grandchildren. She still puts on the holiday family meals. Burt has been into just about everything in his career that has to do with engineering and general mechanical know-how except, he claims, plumbing and cars—and the latter only because it is "too greasy." After listing the various occupations he has engaged in over the years in the Athol area, he remarked that he is now fascinated by the new possibilities of reproducing photographs on the computer, and he is working with their artist-photographer son and his friend on developing more durable computer inks.

Burt's curiosity about how things work and might work has not abated with his years. Incidentally, neither has his sense of humor. He and Alice enjoy a most amusing repartee, full of quips and surprises.

Filling one's days and living longer are not the only benefits of structured work. It gives our lives some meaning, day by day. Dr. Bortz puts it well.

> The glory of action rests in its delivery of a sense of self-control, and participation, and meaning. It is involvement. An attitude which cries out, "I matter!"
>
> [Bortz, p. 101]

For the very old and infirm, a purpose to get up in the morning may be outside their reach, and yet they have to get up and live through another day, hopefully with a minimum of loneliness, boredom, and depression. For them, the

---

Activities to be Incorporated into a Routine

- some form of work, so that other activities become "play"
- three regular meals and a planned snack or two
- whatever exercise is possible for a stated amount of time
- phone calls and letters to friends
- one or more naps as needed, at regular times
- reading of some sort for at least an hour
- whatever television programs are interesting
- some type of hand work if sight allows

benefits of a daily routine cannot be overemphasized. I have been appalled at the lack of any routine in the lives of most of the "old old" whom I visit.

Lacking a reason to do anything at any one time, some get their night's sleep at times other than the night, such as between 9 a.m. and 12 p.m. and then from 7 p.m. to 1 a.m. Eating is often irregular. Soap operas provide for some the only structure in their daily lives. When bored, they wonder what to do and notice how bored they are. But a daily routine, once developed, can provide enough structure to decrease boredom greatly.

My friend Lucille is far and away the most bored and depressed person I have known. She is a widow of eighty-five with a very sweet and winning little voice. When I enter her apartment, I always find her curled up on her sofa watching a soap opera or game show. As she clicks off the television, she begins telling me that she feels awful, that she has never felt worse, that people don't believe that she always feels worse, and that the doctor has again changed her medication but it is making her sicker. "And what is wrong?" I politely ask, as if I didn't know, because her response does not vary. Her body burns and hurts all over from the top to the bottom, with a new pressure on the top of her head, worse than ever before.

The doctors—and she has seen them all—can find nothing physically wrong with Lucille except high blood pressure and occasional minor ailments. She can walk around her apartment and with a bit of help can go out. She is able to cook her own meals, although she does have a meal delivered at noon. Her hearing is poor, but she is physically in pretty good shape. The medical diagnosis of her condition is mental depression, for which she takes one medication after another, apparently without effect.

All Lucille does is watch television with a cigarette in her mouth, sprawl scantily dressed day and night on the couch, telephone the doctor's office and the pharmacy, and contrive to get services from one or another of her eight children in the area as well as from all possible agencies. She refuses to go to a senior center or any group gathering, saying that she only enjoys seeing her family. Her conversation is almost totally about her illness, with some updating about the goings on of her family. Occasionally I can push her into coming with me for a cup of coffee and even get her to think very, very briefly about something besides herself. Often I can tease her into laughing, sometimes about her own canniness in cadging services. I offer her the assurance that I care about her—which somehow or other I do—and an hour of diversion. Nevertheless, I leave wondering whether I have wasted an hour.

Lucille has slipped into the black hole bit by bit throughout her life, caring for no one but herself and now terribly afraid of dying. She will only talk briefly

Suggestions to Alleviate Depression

Always dress as if you are expecting company. I have found that when I have neglected to apply lipstick and brushed back my hair too quickly, I have less self-respect. As I pass by my mirror, I look at myself and express opinions that I do not enjoy hearing. However, once I comb my hair neatly, carefully put on some lipstick, and slip into an attractive shirt, I feel like a different and decidedly more upbeat person. A simple remedy, but useful in my own life. I encourage my elderly friends to keep up their personal appearance through praise when they do and surprise when they don't.

Put your affairs in order. This suggestion means different things to different people, but it always includes a properly executed will. Once this is done, it is easier to ignore the possibility of an imminent death and think of the future as stretching out ahead. It allows you to concentrate on living fully now rather than preparing to die for the rest of your life.

Make plans for the future. Doing so not only provides activity to anticipate with pleasure, but also gives a sense of time ahead with specific dates, thus helping to distract from any feeling of simply getting through the day in the same old way.

Develop the habit of expecting something wonderful to happen, just around the corner. It often does, and it always does eventually. If you are expecting the wonderful thing, you are more likely to recognize it and appreciate it when it happens. Nothing is lost while you are waiting for it, and the pleasure of anticipation is gained. I have found this very helpful during difficult periods in my own life.

about it, but the fear of death comes up at least once during the hour I spend with her. As a counselor, I encourage her to talk about her past life and pull it together in her own mind, but because she has led a life of which she disapproves, she seems to feel all the more depressed.

In an effort to help Lucille and other homebound people, I have suggested following a routine such as those on page 109.

From observing and trying to help the depressed elders I visit, I have gleaned a few other practical suggestions that, along with routine, may help relieve daily depression for us all. I have found that little acts with no apparent deep psychological import can often be almost miraculous bootstraps for pulling onself back from the edge of the deep, dark hole. Suggestions appear above.

Sarton offers similar ideas in her last book, *At Eighty-Two: A Journal,* where she writes of the little techniques she herself was finding useful to combat her recurrent depression. They include changing her clothes, tidying things, and making quick meals. Maggie Kuhn agrees on the last of my suggestions, telling how she looks for the surprises in life.

> And every day, every day is some surprise. I look for that. What's going to be new, what's new today? There is seldom a day without some element of surprise. I think in a sense surprise is synonymous with hope.
>
> [Kuhn, *Ageless*, p. 129]

Such suggestions for alleviating depression will not pull anyone back who has already slipped far into the "deep, dark hole." They have not helped Lucille, who is beyond even paying attention, much less trying to follow them. They can be useful for some of us in the fight against depression but cannot completely conquer this rightly dreaded condition. As discussed earlier, depression like Lucille's is often a response to awareness of one's mortality and all that it entails spiritually. Sarton writes gloomily,

> There are no quick rewards for the depressed person. It is a matter of making a channel and then guiding one's boat through it, day by day. For me, the channel has always been work.
>
> [Sarton, *Plant*, p. 87]

Suggestions given above are not only for my "old old" friends, but for myself and others among the "young old." It is time for us to prepare, so that we may avoid the ever-lurking trio of loneliness, boredom, and depression. And one very important but often neglected way is to develop the ability to derive deep enjoyment from a number of usually solitary occupations open to us all, regardless of age.

Acquiring Ageless Pleasures

In writing about the necessity to maintain and initiate interaction with other people as one grows older, I quoted Scott-Maxwell on the strong need for occasional solitude. While she writes of using solitude for introspection and facing basic life questions, there are many other ways to spend time alone fruitfully and contentedly, from childhood on.

As we age, the world tends to become smaller for us. If we live long enough, we will lose the physical ability to do many things we have previously enjoyed and that have given us a sense of worth. Previous pleasures requiring physical strength or companions will gradually become impossible for us. We will often be alone, because our mates and close friends may die before us and we will no longer be able to go to other people. Scott-Maxwell speaks of the way in which the multiple losses of the very old restrict their world.

> When you have to accept loss, you know you are retreating on to less and less territory. The play of your heart will be restricted, the area of your interest lessened. The territory of the old is very small, and it hurts to diminish.
>
> [Scott-Maxwell, pp. 44-45]

We may spend our final years with almost nothing to do, no one to be with, and nothing to think about. Unless, that is, we have learned to partake of the "ageless pleasures" that keep the world open to us, even when alone. They are ageless both because we can enjoy them throughout our lives and because they are not lessened—but in fact may be increased—by our having lived many years.

Freya Stark describes how such pleasures can give joy to the sensitive heart and mind.

> On the whole, age comes most gently to those who have some doorway into an abstract world—art, or philosophy, or learning—regions where the years are scarcely noticed and young and old can meet in a pale truthful light.
>
> [Stark, *Songs*, p. 329]

For Stark, these pleasures of what she terms the "abstract world" are wonderful because not only may they be enjoyed at any age but also they may be shared with people of any age. When I visited with the artist Barbara Ellis, she attributed a measure of what I termed her "successful aging" to her many youthful friends, most of whom share her keen interest in the visual arts. Interaction with other people can be and often is a by-product of the ability to enjoy the "ageless pleasures."

Stark believes that the perspective as well as losses that come with age may enlarge our spiritual receptiveness.

> We move there [in the abstract world] with increasing freedom as Time rubs out the illusions of possession, whose dark attendant, envy, fades away. The loss of our own things, or such we thought so, our faculties, our friends, our loves—makes us again receptive as in childhood, though now it is no human hand that gives. In our increasing poverty, the universal riches grow more apparent, the careless showering of gifts regardless of return; our private grasp lessens, and leaves us heirs to infinite loves in a common world where every joy is a part of one's personal joy.
>
> [Stark, *Songs*, p. 329]

Perhaps the most available solitary "abstract" pleasure is reading. Books are, in effect, an open window that allows us to leave our own little room and for a brief period live in a wider world. We visit with the author, learning about what is, has been, or might have been. On our return, we are refreshed and more ready to take up what may be a constricted and burdensome life. Sarton often speaks eloquently of what books meant to her during her periods of illness or depression. In *Endgame*, she writes,

> It is strange that I have not spoken of what I have been reading this lamentable spring, for books are what have kept me alive. They and the English weeklies, . . . and a long read every day of the *New York Times*, keep me aware of the world beyond this safe green-and-blue enclosure.
>
> [Sarton, *Endgame*, p. 33]

> Parts of me are simply not operating. I feel about a fifth here as far as who May Sarton *was*. . . . So I read with enormous enjoyment still but it's the only thing that I do perhaps at full blast—.
>
> [Sarton, *Endgame*, p. 181]

The actress Helen Hayes views the opportunity to read as one of the greatest gifts of her old age and an antidote to loneliness as well.

> There were many times in my life, until I was left alone, that I wished for solitude. I now find that I love solitude. I never had the blessed gift of being alone until the last of my loved ones was wrested from me. Now I can go sometimes for days and days without seeing anyone. I'm not entirely alone, because I listen to the radio and read the newspapers. I love to read. That is my greatest new luxury, having the time to read.
>
> [Hayes, *Songs*, p. 279]

An unidentified correspondent writes enthusiastically to Boyd

> When I'm reading, when I'm really absorbed in a wonderful book, the sort of pleasure I feel is ageless—it occurs in a kind of dreamtime where the me who's reacting never changes. It's the only fountain of youth I've found.
>
> [Boyd, August 13]

Scott-Maxwell finds some of her happiness in rereading:

> One of the pleasures of age is reading books long forgotten, with only the enlargement they once brought remembered.
>
> [Scott-Maxwell, p. 99]

Another of the "ageless pleasures" is music. Although I personally am not in any sense musical, I would feel very deprived if I were to live day after day without hearing any classical music. I expected to find a wealth of testimony in the literature to the value of music as a pleasure available to all at least through recordings, but I found almost nothing on the subject.

Then it occurred to me that perhaps the value of music to the old is too obvious to write about. Nursing homes these days usually try to include sing-alongs and musical performances in their list of activities. Even people with considerable hearing loss are able to perceive enough of the sound to respond positively

Ralph Hills, the author's husband, practices daily on his beloved baby grand piano.

to music. The close link of music with remembrances may be the primary reason for the pleasure old people derive from it. A second reason is, of course, enjoyment of the music for itself, whether it be jazz, classical music, rock and roll, country music, or folk songs.

Sarton provides the only clear testimony to the value of music that I found in books.

> Now at this moment Mozart (the Piano Concerto in G Major, no. 17) is pouring energy into my spirit like a cordial.
>
> [Sarton, *At Seventy*, p. 119]

> Now I am playing something I have thought of listening to for days. Chausson's Symphony in B-Flat. . . . As I listen I am at last back in myself after days of frustration and fear of dying. So tired is my heart that I did not know what to do with myself.
>
> [Sarton, *Encore*, p. 274]

She also offers a testimony to various ageless pleasures that includes music.

> One thing is certain, and I have always known it—the joys of my life have nothing to do with age. They do not change. Flowers, the morning and evening light, music, poetry, silence, the goldfinches darting about . . .
>
> [Sarton, *At Seventy*, p. 17]

One of the persons I interviewed, without a question or suggestion from me on the subject, brought up music as a pleasure that she could enjoy if she were one day to find herself alone and homebound. Elsa Bakalar, the double-passioned gardener mentioned earlier, said that she had so much music and poetry in her memory that she would be able to spend many hours just listening to them both run through her mind. As I heard this, I wished that my memory held equal treasures.

Although Sarton speaks of the value of music in her later years, she does not mention art. And I found no written rhapsody to art as a major source of interest or pleasure in old age. Stark includes it in the quote above about the value of being able to inhabit an abstract world but does not further elaborate.

The scarcity of tributes to art as an ageless pleasure might be attributed to its not being, like music and literature, an occupation that has to involve a particular period of time and thus does not take us away from our daily life for an hour or so. Yet I would think that the enjoyment of gazing at a picture, enjoying its balance, colour, and line, perhaps entering into its world if it is at least somewhat representational or suggests depth, would tend to increase as we settle down a bit and have more time to enjoy such things. Particularly if the art is familiar.

The "ageless pleasures," those that may survive and become important in the later years, seem to divide themselves into the more intellectual or cultural ones discussed above and those deriving from nature—flowers, pets, and birds.

Unfortunately, only a few of the older people whom I visit as counselor or companion are able to find stimulation and refreshment from the first category of reading, music, or art, and those few tend to read romance novels or perhaps news stories in the daily paper, but rarely any writing with substantial intellectual or spiritual content. When I suggest reading as a pastime or bring books that I think might interest, the response is usually, "I have never been a reader," with the implication that it is too late to start now.

Nor have I found much interest in music or art. Most entertainment comes from television, primarily soap operas and quiz shows. While these help to prevent the world from narrowing completely, their ability to stimulate the intellect or refresh and enliven the spirit is minimal.

I have found much more participation in the "ageless pleasures" of nature. Enjoyment of flowers does not seem to lessen. Perhaps it increases as other pleasures decrease. For those who are still physically able to go outside and dig in the ground, gardening often seems to be a particular pleasure. Sarton writes many times about the healing effects of working in a garden.

> I set aside all this turbulence yesterday afternoon and planted the eleven lilies needed to replace those the chipmunks ate last winter. It was good to forget everything else and feel the good damp earth in my hands, the great restorer!
>
> [Sarton, *At Seventy*, p. 59]

> I find I have energy in the garden that I cannot summon for anything else.
>
> [Sarton, *Encore*, p. 43]

The film actor, Eddie Albert, states the value of gardening and nature succinctly.

> I'm not altogether sure that I know a whole lot of things, but what I do know is that to lose contact with nature is like throwing gold in the sea and losing it. To have, for example, my lovely garden here every day and not get out in it is a crime.
>
> [Albert, *Ageless*, p. 21]

Of course, I asked Elsa Bakalar, expert gardener, about whether her gardening could be considered an ageless pleasure. She had mentioned in her book that older people in particular enjoy gardens not only for the beauty of the plants but for their associations. Individual plants were put in at special times in their lives or given to them by long-gone friends. They bring back pleasant memories.

I knew that for Elsa gardening had been ageless in the sense that she shared this pleasure with many younger people in her workshops. But I wondered how ageless her gardening might be in the other sense—whether it would be able to help her if she were homebound and alone. She smiled, remembering, and then answered that yes, she thought it would. She told me that when she and her husband lived in New York City, she became very lonely for her gardens, which she had planted at their summer cottage in Heath, at the northernmost part of central Massachusetts. At those times in the city, she would close her eyes and mentally stroll around each garden, thinking about the flowers that already were there and those that possibly she could plant there next season. She found great comfort in doing so, and she thought that such a pleasure would be possible for her in the future if needed.

Even when we can no longer dig and weed in the garden, the sight of flowers provides a lift. When I bring a small bouquet of flowers to one of my older friends, particularly when they were grown in my own quite humble garden, I perceive an inner smile that I believe derives from the sight of the flowers themselves even more than from the affection expressed by them.

Another gift of nature rather than of the intellect that I have found much appreciated by the elderly is the presence of an animal. Just the sight of a dog or cat brought for a moment into a nursing home can bring the same type of inner smile onto the faces of some older people. Stroking or caressing that animal obviously increases the pleasure. I mentioned earlier that for persons still able to live in their own homes, pets help to assuage loneliness and provide a simple but effective purpose for getting up in the morning and "keeping going" in their own home. They also offer the tactile sensations of touching another living creature that are so often absent in the life of the "old old." Again, from Sarton:

I spent the day in acute pain lying on my bed. At such times Pierrot, who turns over on his back to be caressed, is a great comfort. His big flossy paws never put claws out and his soft tummy is a pleasure to stroke.

[Sarton, *Endgame*, p. 37]

[about letting the cat in and out at night] —if I have to do it three times a night, each time waking up from a deep sleep, it is costly. Often I don't get to sleep again. However, he's worth it. Without some living thing in the house it would become too lonely, too lonely for words, too lonely for silence. I would just, I'm afraid, cry. So he is a delight in spite of what he costs me.

[Sarton, *Endgame*, p. 101]

Pierrot is a great comfort. The sight of his soft, glossy coat as he lies on the end of the bed is somehow health-giving.

[Sarton, *Endgame*, p. 171]

Watching birds—as apart from the quite active sport of "birdwatching"—is another pleasure often available to the "old old" in nursing homes. And the more they already know about birds, the more they are able to enjoy the behavior patterns of different species. For the elderly still in their own homes, birds can be a very special pleasure. Several of "my" older ladies are very diligent in maintaining bird feeders within sight of their special chair, which always faces the television as well as the window. They will give me news of any unusual birds they have seen during the week, but the real enthusiasm seems to be directed toward the squirrels, who are without fail viewed as the enemy. I remember with amusement entering the trailer home of one woman in her eighties who was holding a BB gun out the window. With great gusto she told me about her success in frightening off a particularly nervy squirrel that day and of her long, but as yet unsuccessful, fight against the squirrels who were "raiding" her four bird feeders.

Not all of the enjoyment comes from fighting the ever-present squirrels. Most of the elderly I know just enjoy watching the birds come and go, squabble, and feed. I was delighted to find a poem about how curative this simple pleasure can become. It was written by Mona Van Duyn, editor and poet, in *Letters from a Father*.

The first part of the letter consists solely of physical complaints. The second part mentions only a few aches and pains, but is very pessimistic.

> We enjoyed your visit, it was nice of you to bring
> the feeder but a terrible waste of your money
> for that big bag of feed since we won't be living
> more than a few weeks longer. . . .

[Van Duyn, *Songs*, p. 136}

In the next three parts, the father writes almost completely about the birds in his yard, with almost nothing about his or his wife's illness. He says that they bought a bird book and he writes about all the amusing antics of the different kinds. The sixth begins with

> It's sure a surprise how well Mother is doing,

and continues

> . . . I am going to keep
> feeding all spring, maybe summer, you can see
> they expect it. . . .

[Van Duyn, *Songs*, p. 138]

One realizes that he no longer believes that he and his wife will die in the immediate future. The touching and beautiful comment after the letter is this:

> So the world woos its children back for an evening kiss.

[Van Duyn, *Songs*, p. 138]

Responding Spiritually

Finding Meaning in Life

Valuable and necessary as purposeful and creative work, along with routine, may be in our lives as we age, there is another type of "work" that cannot be forgotten and that becomes increasingly important. I refer to the effort to find meaning in our lives, to figure out where we have been and why, and at last to discover who we really are in universal terms. Fortunately, such an endeavor becomes natural to us as we continue to develop, often in conjunction with the remembering and musing discussed earlier as one of the "joys."

The initial stage of this type of work is "remembrance," in LeShan's definition of the word. The complex changes in our memories lead us as we age to muse about our past. Old age is a time when we tend to forget the trivial of the present day in favor of remembering what has happened to us and what we have done earlier, in an attempt to understand our lives as a whole. It becomes our appropriate and necessary work. LeShan phrases it well.

> I am learning, slowly but surely, that *remembrance of things past* is the necessary work of my brain as I get older, so that I know more clearly each day just what makes me, as a person, as special and unique as my fingerprints.

[LeShan, *50 Again*, p. 78]

She continues with the theme later in the same chapter, emphasizing the spiritual aspect of the work.

> There is another aspect of remembrance that has a more profound meaning, going far beyond the issue of personal identity. While we may be forgetting some of the details of daily living, and some peripheral facts, we aren't remembering only the past. What we are remembering are matters of universal importance—things that have to do with the quality of our lives. We are thinking more about loving; we are remembering those experiences that make us feel part of nature, part of the larger universe—a magnificent sunset, a mother bird feeding her babies. We look more closely into the heart of some exquisite flower. We are capable of becoming more reflective, more contemplative. *Being human and being part of a larger universe* is a natural and necessary developmental task.
>
> [LeShan, *50 Again,* pp. 79-80]

Eventually, LeShan believes that the effort to find meaning in life may lead to acceptance of our death.

> The more successful we are in distilling what is really important about life, the more accepting we will become of our mortality. We are moving slowly from the specifics of daily living to the larger issue of the meaning of our lives.
>
> [LeShan, *50 Again,* p. 80]

Although none of the old people I visit has said anything even faintly resembling the above quotation, most seem to be doing just about what it says, and doing it very naturally and unselfconsciously. Like many of the elderly, they are ready and willing at the slightest sign of interest to tell and retell the stories of their lives, trying to pull it all together. Occasionally, I see an acceptance of life and death in small phrases, such as the one Mildred uses after complaining about her pains and the doctors' inability to rid her of them. With a big, beautiful smile, she will shrug and toss off the problem at hand with, "Oh well. What can you do? You can't win." And she laughs and changes the subject to something more cheerful.

I see a search for meaning in Jane's stories about her family, past and present, as she tries to find her own place there and to distinguish elements of love and interconnection in the saga. And Lucille, the depressed lady always lying on the couch, in the middle of talk about her ailments, will often suddenly turn to the question haunting her: "Is God going to punish me? Will I go to Hell?" In more philosophical language, "Where do I fit into the universal scheme?"

Lucille seems to be an example of an unsuccessful struggle with the issue of mortality that is described as the cause of much late-life depression in an *Atlantic Monthly* article cited earlier. Each of us tries to find an answer in terms of our view of the world, which differs widely with each person. But all of the elderly people I visit seem to be doing this hard but necessary work in their own way and, from what I can judge, most of them are doing it rather well.

Vivid quotations abound concerning the fascinating late-life task of finding meaning. We will begin with the very verbal and introspective Scott-Maxwell, who predictably takes on the task enthusiastically.

> Now that I am sure this freedom is the right garnering of age I am so busy being old that I dread interruptions. This sense of vigour and spaciousness may cease, and I must enjoy it while it is here.
>
> [Scott-Maxwell, p. 141]

Cowley comes at the same experience from a slightly different angle, pointing out the inappropriateness of tackling the job earlier.

> More and more the older person is driven back into himself; more and more he is occupied with what goes on in his mind. . . . In middle age that absorption in the self had been a weakness to be avoided, a failure to share and participate that ended by diminishing the self. For the very old it becomes a pursuit appropriate to their stage in life. It is still their duty to share affection and contribute to the world as much as possible, but they also have the task of finding and piecing together their personalities.
>
> [Cowley, p. 55]

He continues this thought a bit later, as a writer trying to find a plot.

> One project among many, one that tempts me and might be tempting to others, is trying to find a shape or pattern in our life. There are such patterns, I believe, even if they are hard to discern. Our lives that seemed a random and monotonous series of incidents are something more than that; each of them has a plot.
>
> [Cowley, pp. 70-71]

Author Barbara Myerhoff writes of an epiphanous experience, saying that memory

> may offer opportunity not merely to recall the past but to relive it, in all its original freshness, unaltered by intervening changes and reflections. Such magical Proustian moments are pinpoints of the greatest intensity, when a sense of the past never being truly lost is experienced. . . . Often such moments involve childhood memories, and then one experiences the self as it was originally, and knows beyond doubt that one is the same person as that child who still dwells within a time-altered body. Integration through memory with earlier states of being surely provides the sense of continuity and completeness that may be counted as an essential developmental task of old age.
>
> [Myerhoff, *Oxford*, pp. 382-83]

She describes what she calls "re-membering," a term she attributes to Victor Turner, and continues,

> The focused unification provided by Re-membering is requisite to sense and order. Through it, a life is given shape that extends back in the past and forward into the future, a simplified, edited tale where completeness may be sacrificed for moral and aesthetic purposes.
>
> [Myerhoff, *Oxford*, p. 383]

Remembrance is beautifully described by Julius Lester in the novel, *Do Lord Remember Me*, where an old black minister muses about and relives the past in an attempt to understand what his life has meant. Lester writes,

> Since the stroke he had begun walking across the landscape of the past.

For Rev. Joshua Smith

> there was no clean separation between sleep and wakefulness any longer.

He considers his remembrance of all that had happened.

> The past was an actuality whose detail and reality could not be seen and examined when it was present. Only now, when there was nothing but past, did it surface to be examined and lived truly for the first time. When past was all, present was all, and there were no uncertainties and anxieties because the resolution was known.
>
> [Lester, p. 101]

Later he realizes that his contemplation of the past has indeed brought him understanding and peace.

> We don't know who we are, he thought, until we turn and look back at who we were. That's why Death wasn't nothing but a walk into the Light which would take him in and warm him and hide him and let him rest after working in the vineyard of the Lord. There was nothing to fear when you could see all the way back like he could now.
>
> [Lester, p. 179]

Development continues until the end in a successful completion of the work of old age.

Scott-Maxwell also seems to have come to an understanding of herself and her life during her later years.

> Age is a desert of time—hours, days, weeks, years perhaps—with little to do. So one has ample time to face everything one has had, been, done; gather them all in: the things that came from outside, and those from inside. We have time at last to make them truly ours.
>
> [Scott-Maxwell, p. 41]

She also thinks an acceptance of death is one of the rewards of her work at understanding her life.

> You need only claim the events of your life to make yourself yours. When you truly possess all you have been and done, which may take some time, you are fierce with reality. When at last age has assembled you together, will it not be easy to let it all go, lived, balanced, over?
>
> [Scott-Maxwell, p. 42]

Not everyone enters willingly into the work. Somewhat to my surprise, Sarton writes in her seventy-eighth year, concerning the interviews by her future biographer,

> It is a stressful time, and I am beginning to realize why. It is at least in part because I am being forced to look back on my life, and the way to live well when you are eighty is to live in the present and the future. I do not want to look back, but because Margot Peters is writing my biography, she naturally asks questions, and I am forced to look back. She has left me very much alone, but the fact that she is thinking about my life makes me come to terms with it. She brought up the name of the first woman I ever shared an apartment with, and now I have to think about that and what I should say. It brings everything back, you see, and what I really want is to look out at the gray sea through the falling snow.
>
> [Sarton, *Encore*, p. 213]

In contradiction, however, she had written earlier in the same journal.

> I feel a wild excitement at being alone again. I feel like an armadillo all curled up in a shiny ball. The fact is that nothing interests me as much, perhaps, as myself at this stage of my life. I have so much to think about.
>
> [Sarton, *Encore*, p. 168]

Reminiscing in a journal offers a chance to reflect, muse, and ponder. The elderly may keep journals not simply by handwriting or typing—both good vehicles for the process— but also by computer. The computer also offers vast Internet resources and practical applications like checkbook maintenance and databasing files.

While musing and remembering are one way of ferreting out the meaning of one's life, making entries into a journal or a diary is another major approach for persons to whom writing comes easily, regardless of age. Knowing the benefits of journal writing particularly for older people, communities for the elderly often sponsor classes in the art.

May Sarton provides an outstanding recent example of someone who depended upon her daily writing as a way of discovering the meaning of her own life. She said again and again how essential her journal was to her peace of mind:

> I feel happy to be keeping a journal again. I have missed it, missed "naming things" as they appear, missed the half hour when I push all duties aside and savor the experience of being alive in this beautiful place.
>
> [Sarton, *At Seventy*, p. 17]

> Still, I find that keeping a journal again validates and clarifies. For the hour I manage in the morning at this task I am happy, at ease with myself and the world, even when I am complaining of pressure.
>
> [Sarton, *At Seventy*, p. 50]

She writes of

> discovering what is really happening to me by keeping a journal.
>
> [Sarton, *Encore*, p. 11]

Near the end of her seventies, when she had to dictate rather than type, Sarton still saw the value of the journal.

> I do think keeping a journal, even if it has to be spoken instead of written, is good medicine. It makes me sort out what's important in my life now.
>
> [Sarton, *End*, p. 65]

Scott-Maxwell refers to her journal as "a notebook," but she obviously derived some of the same benefits from it as did Sarton from her journal.

> A note book might be the very thing for all the old who wave away crossword puzzles, painting, petit point, and knitting. It is more restful than conversation, and for me it has become a companion, more, a confessional. It cannot shrive me, but knowing myself better comes near to that.
>
> [Scott-Maxwell, p. 65]

Australian Ellen Newton, writing in her eighty-third year from a less than adequate nursing home, says that she started keeping a journal at the amusingly stern advice of a friend:

> *Tuesday*   A writer, whose beautifully perceptive essays and letters are cherished by people lucky enough to own them, once asked me if I kept a diary. My answer was "No."
> "Begin today," she said in her clipped, clear voice.
> Often I've wished I had taken her advice long ago. A diary cannot blush. It will let you unwind—without audible comment. My present safety valve is this rather scruffy, well-used notebook complete with ballpoint pen. If you must search your heart, better to put

in your time writing of what you find there, than wasting your days wallowing in wretchedness.

[Newton, Oxford, p. 157]

I can personally attest to the value of journal writing. My move from the suburbs of Washington, D.C. up to rural Massachusetts occurred within the same year as my remarriage and my retirement. Add to those three big changes another which to me seemed almost as daunting—starting to care for my own horses for the first time in my life. Realizing that some stress would be involved, I started retreating each evening after dinner to my computer. There I would first note briefly the major events of the day and then discuss my problems on paper. After a year or so, I was able to find threads in each of the challenges that enabled me to pull it all together as a story of how one sixty-two-year-old woman handled four simultaneous big changes in her life. Journal writing put the difficulties I faced into a larger context and helped me see more clearly where I had been and where I was going.

A third approach to finding meaning in life seems to be favored by Friedan. She adds an element of the future to our attempts to discover the meaning of our lives. She calls it "generativity."

> There seems to me to be a need in later years to see our lives as part of a larger whole—the stream of life that will go on after our death. This includes not just our children and grandchildren but also the trees we plant that will bloom after we die, the causes we advance that will make the world better.
>
> [Friedan, Parade Magazine, p. 6]

Arnold Toynbee at seventy-five wrote,

> Every human being is a Janus. 'We look before and after.' . . . If one were to fall into this backward-looking stance, one would be as good (I mean as bad) as dead. Lord Russell is reported to have said, when he was already far on in his eighties, that it is important to care immensely about things that are going to happen after one is dead. All ageing people ought to make this saying their own, and to act on it, as Lord Russell has done. Our minds, so long as they keep their cutting edge, are not bound by our physical limits; they can range over time and space into infinity. To be human is to be capable of transcending oneself.
>
> [Toynbee, Oxford, p. 369]

Friedan believes that the example older people can give now and the social actions they can take to improve the world for their children and grandchildren are major elements in this generativity.

> And through our actions, we will create a new image of age—free and joyous, living with pain, saying what we really think and feel at last—knowing who we are, realizing that we know more than we ever knew we knew, not afraid of what anyone thinks of us anymore, moving with wonder into that unknown future we have helped shape for generations coming after us.
>
> [Friedan, Time, p. 64]

A different experience of generativity, a more mystical one, is expressed vividly by author Carter Catlett Williams, in the simple act of baking a custard for a sick friend and remembering how this had been done for her by her mother.

> Then for an indelible moment I was my mother and my child self: in an out-of-time meshing of the joy of giving and receiving, I was at once the receiving child and the giving mother. Somehow I was mother, child, my mother, myself, Giver and Receiver.
>
> This shining moment in my kitchen sends shafts of light across my days. . . .
>
> Now my daughter is intent on making her father's birthday cake while her daughter makes contented sounds in her bouncing seat nearby. Through all the generations, through all the days and years, the giving and receiving continue to weave the very fabric of our lives, and we find ourselves in each other and in all ages.
>
> [Williams, *Oxford*, pp. 132-33]

Moving toward Blessedness

I use the term "blessedness" here to mean that state of mind, heart, and soul that would be most joyous for each individual. Although everyone longs for it, we each have our own way of imagining it, defining it, and trying to achieve it. This section deals with the possible spiritual movement of an individual as death approaches, either over a long period of time for the very old whose bodies are wearing out slowly or over a short period for those whose bodies are succumbing to a lingering but fatal disease.

Sybil Harton, the English writer who will be quoted extensively in this section, sees life in religious terms and writes accordingly. If your thought patterns are not religious, I ask you not to be put off by Harton's way of expressing herself, but to translate from her pattern of thought to your own, which can be readily done with a bit of imagination and empathy. The substance of what Harton writes is worth the effort.

I should point out, however, that Harton's comments, perceptive and inspiring as they are, partake of the quality of a novel. She is intuiting, imagining, on the basis of her own spiritual experiences and perhaps of her reading, what approaching death might be like at its spiritual best. Her book was probably written in her late middle age, so she has obviously not herself experienced what she is describing.

The following lines stand at the beginning of Harton's *On Growing Old—A Preparation for Age.*

> May your old age be like the evergreen pine
> And its fragrance like the flower of the red camellia.
>
> A Chinese wish.

She explains,

> What must constitute the essence of the fragrance of age, namely, the pure condition of being rather than doing; and the simpler this state of "I am," the stronger its quality of love, for pure Being is Love.
>
> [Harton, p. 124]

"Being rather than doing." LeShan, writing this time at the age of sixty-seven, reaches virtually the same conclusion, but in language more accessible to the nonreligious.

> What we are doing is coming closer to the meditative state that might well make our deaths easier to face. We are steadily moving from the world of *Doing* to the world of *Being*. We want to feel that we are part of nature and that nature is a part of us—that there is a larger universe beyond the traffic, the noise, the stress and strain of our daily lives.
>
> [LeShan, *Hill*, p. 25]

The movement from doing to being is the key to Harton's approach to one of the situations that many people fear, dependence, and two of what I have termed the major problems, loneliness and boredom. She does not mention the third, depression. The fact that she discusses several of the problems that I have observed in so many older people made my discovery of her rather obscure little book even more fortuitous. Harton sees all the difficulties as God's way of preparing our souls to accept His Spirit more completely as we approach death.

Regarding dependence, Harton acknowledges that it is particularly offensive to some natures.

> To be under an obligation to another person is often, and for some natures, so much more difficult than conferring benefits, to receive service may be much harder than giving it; but maybe we are brought to old age especially to acquire this docility.
>
> [Harton, p. 90]

Nevertheless, we must accept dependence and do so cheerfully and wholeheartedly.

> But do not let us merely resign ourselves to make the best of a bad job, there is no sweetness in that sort of mind, for resignation by itself turns sour. Rather, we go forward with both hands outstretched to take whatever conditions God decrees, and to like them, positively like them, because they are His will.
>
> [Harton, p. 89]

To Harton, dependence accepted cheerfully actually confers freedom.

> Moreover, by going willingly and contentedly towards whatever state of helplessness may be our lot, we actually preserve and foster interior freedom, which belongs to the inward life for which we now have time. But all this acquiescence must begin long before we reach old age.
>
> [Harton, p. 91]

On loneliness, Harton writes that it can be "good"—

when one uses it in preparation for the departure from this world for another . . . For this loneliness is a blessed file which by a sure, if painful, process, removes all that attaches us to our fellows, gradually refining our emotions and our desires until they are unified into a point which is pure love, simple charity, one with that love which is God.

[Harton, p. 81]

She goes directly on with a particularly perceptive observation about the ego.

Even more, I have to attain detachment from myself. I am to go to God our Home as I truly am in my naked self, and how much of me is facade, an exterior, additional front which I have built up between myself and my fellow-men, between myself and myself, in order to impress, to gain attention and credit from, not necessarily the others so much as, myself.

[Harton, p. 81]

Loneliness becomes for Harton actually a gift of God.

He in his wonderful mercy provides this blessed time of age to scrape away the false fronts. . . . Blessed loneliness, which comes open-armed, smiling, laden with gifts. In the quiet and the silence we have no longer to be less than ourselves, no more need we speak thoughtlessly, aimlessly, anxiously: gone are the emotional upheavals and the tempests of passion, and in inner peace and stillness the soul can expand and grow in ways hitherto undreamt of, drinking deeply at the springs of pure being.

[Harton, p. 82]

As the ego is worn away, as the self no longer blocks God's Spirit, the lonely person becomes filled with love for others and is indeed blessed.

And as you open your heart more and more to Him (for there is now no one else to open it to), you are able to be filled with His love which flows through you to embrace all men. Slowly it works but surely, so that there comes a time when no person is any longer distasteful to you, none misunderstood, none a nuisance. Your love desires great goodness for them all and, as you become a deep well of charity which shuts out no one, it ministers unseen to an unknown multitude. . . . No need to wait for old age for this, we begin to desire and to practise it at any age, but the circumstances of Age may bring it to perfection.

[Harton, p. 83]

In the introduction to the chapter on "Solitude/Loneliness," the editors of *The Oxford Book of Aging* offer a similar view of loneliness, minus the religious element.

Facing existential aloneness without the essential social masks and conventions that define our public selves, can be a terrifying experience. Yet it is filled with potential for deepening self-knowledge, cultivating loving relationships, and soulfully accepting mortality.

[Cole and Winkler, *Oxford*, p. 149]

Poet Siegfried Sassoon writes of this stripping of all but the basics from our souls.

When I Am Alone

"When I'm alone"—The words tripped off his tongue
As though to be alone were nothing strange.
'When I was young,' he said, *'when I was young. . . .'*
I thought of age, and loneliness, and change.
I thought how strange we grow when we're alone,
And how unlike the selves that meet, and talk,
And blow the candles out, and say good-night.
Alone . . . The word is life endured and known.
It is the stillness where our spirits walk
And all but inmost faith is overthrown.

[Sassoon, *Oxford*, pp. 150-51]

On another problem of very old age, boredom, Harton perceives that even the enforced inactivity may produce love toward others.

Gently and softly our last years teach us to brood rather than bustle, and if the eyes are blind we learn to see with the heart. It is the slowness and patience of the old which provide just that tranquillity and security which children seek, and so it is that the old and the young are often contented companions, with mutual sympathy and good will.

[Harton, pp. 91-92]

Tranquility even removes some of the unattractive characteristics often seen in older people, which Harton freely acknowledges.

From this serene contentment they receive the grace not to desire to talk of themselves, to scorn, to be opinionated, such temptations do not come their way anymore.

[Harton, p. 101]

To offset the heaviness of time, Harton gives counsel like that offered by others earlier in this book, namely, a routine that is faithfully followed.

Yet in this trial of the dragging hour, when there seems nothing left to live for, self-discipline remains a solid ally, helping to preserve the personality. Happy are we if we have always accustomed ourselves to order our days in a pattern. . . . In old age our rule will stand us in good stead. Forcing ourselves, as far as ability permits, to have a little programme, to work at some hobby, some interest, to have small and regular responsibilities, to go in and out, even against our inclinations, will help to preserve physical and mental health and maintain vitality.

[Harton, p. 92]

She adds an important religious dimension, with a practical suggestion for the bedridden, reminiscent of certain Eastern practices.

But nothing will provide such steady bedrock happiness as a response to the psalmist's "seven times a day do I praise thee," for seven times may at last be within our compass and make our delight. The very chiming of a clock can mark, not the passing of wearisome hours but the call to an act of worship, however brief, perhaps only one short dart of prayer, a look of love at the Heavenly Father; but a definite look, a definite dart, a definite offering. . . . This way lies true health.

[Harton, p. 92]

When even a semblance of a varied routine becomes impossible, there remains a beautiful "fragrance."

The passing days which seem so long and slow, which are so empty of activity and display, are not useless when they bring this final opportunity for the aged soul to make itself an offering for the needs of the whole world, an offering made by simply being an adherence to love. What riches, what qualities of beauty, what a fragrance borne across creation.

[Harton, p. 125]

We still have a purpose, although much different from those of our active days.

Our days and our lives are not emptied of purpose but there is a change, and when we perceive and accept that, we begin to feel the particular vocation of old age, the mode in which it will attain perfection. . . . The sweet, patient endurance of the humiliations and limitations of decline can be transformed into prayer; for prayer is, far more than words, the offering of the self, a movement of being, which is outwards towards God instead of inwards towards the ego, an orientation of mind and will towards Glory.

[Harton, p. 86]

The "vocation of old age" is part of a natural development.

Being is greater than doing: and though it is essential for growth that being should issue in doing, now has come the time of full achievement, when diversity of doing shall gradually be merged and folded into the unity of being. I am: I do: I am; this is a graph of life.

[Harton, p. 87]

When freely accepted, the vocation of being rather than doing can bring peace.

If day by day we say, "My God, I offer these last days of my life," believing that there is a purpose in that act of giving, the quiet, sedentary inactivity will hold no fret or frustration but a serene, tranquil peace, precious in itself.

[Harton, p. 87]

May Sarton also finds peace near the end of her life, writing in her final journal that she

has grown beyond something, the eternal puzzle, and come into something, the peace of acceptance of reality however painful.

[Sarton, *At Eighty-Two*, p. 28]

In closing this chapter, I can do no better than quote Harton once again, as she combines her straightforward, unvarnished approach to life and religion with the necessity to live well now so that we may be prepared for the many and varied challenges that old age may bring.

> Faith is an acceptance of reality, a reaction to spiritual facts, to truth, the very virtue with which we affirm God, answer Him and live in Him. . . . So when we arrive at our last years and are conscious of being peeled of our personality, we are to know that, though our powers seem all withdrawn, we live truly in the depths of being which has become simply faith: and where there is faith, hope and charity abide also.
>
> [Harton, p. 106]

Or as Grandpa puts it, more succinctly but just as clearly, in *Cold Sassy Tree*:

> "Well'm, faith ain't no magic wand or money-back gar'ntee, either one. Hit's jest a way a-livin'. Hit means you don't worry th'ew the days. Hit means you go'n be holdin' on to God in good or bad times, and you accept whatever happens. Hit means you respect life like it is—like God made it—even when it ain't what you'd order from the wholesale house."
>
> [Burns, *Oxford*, p. 314]

Thoughts on Visiting the Elderly

As long as we think that caring means only being nice and friendly to old people, paying them a visit, bringing them a flower or offering them a ride, we are apt to forget how much more important it is for us to be willing and able to be present to those we care for.

[Nouwen, p. 90]

"Faith is an acceptance of reality," writes Sybil Harton. Her statement expresses succinctly the strong cord that for me connects religion to counseling, whether directed toward myself or others. We are dealing with real life, "even when it ain't what you'd order from the wholesale house," as Grandpa puts it. Real life is what God created and where His all-powerful and compassionate Spirit dwells. Our spiritual work, in a special way as we grow older, is to accept it wholeheartedly and even to celebrate it when we can. Insofar as we succeed, we are happy and even at times joyful.

As a companion and counselor for two local agencies, I visit about ten of their elderly clients weekly or biweekly. Most are above seventy-five years old, and many are in their eighties. My primary aim is indirectly to help my clients to realize—in religious language—that God loves them, as His love flows through me to them; in secular language, that someone cares about them enough to be their friend, to listen to them, and to try to help them for a few hours.

In either language, my secondary aim is to help them realize that their happiness will be increased insofar as they care about other people. Although this "how-to" chapter describes my personal approach as a companion and elder peer counselor, it may be adapted for use by anyone, regardless of age, who wants to bring joy into the life of an elderly person and thus reflected joy into his or her own life.

Terms and Such

I flinch just a bit when I use the word "client." This of course is the term used by the two agencies for which I volunteer, but I usually avoid using it to any of the people I visit because it sounds too cold and businesslike for the relationship I am trying to establish. Here, however, "client" is the most convenient word, so I will use it and try not to flinch. Also, since most of my clients have been women, I will use feminine pronouns so that I can write of them in the singular without the awkward "his/her" phrase.

I have consistently avoided the terminology of the social worker and psychotherapist, believing that clear, everyday language communicates meaning better to more people than does the specialized phraseology used in the profession. While few of my observations—if any—are new, my emphasis and approach are somewhat different from those of professionals. Precisely because they are derived from my particular vantage point as an older counselor and friend, my observations may be more accessible and helpful to other nonprofessionals than would be any learned discussions of psychological theory and practice.

The Relationship

I try to establish a direct relationship between myself and my client—a straight line between our inner selves. This means that I am completely open and honest about myself, thus encouraging the client to be equally so. Because she is the one needing to talk, what is eventually established between us is similar to, but not exactly the same as, a close friendship.

Although I never say this specifically, I am willing and able to stand by our relationship if it develops well. It is thus backed by a real commitment to the client, who usually perceives this subconsciously. My commitment means that I do not stop seeing a client just because she has gone into a nursing home and thus may no longer qualify for a visit under one of my sponsoring agencies. As a retired person whose time is her own, I am able to do this in a way that a busy professional social worker or psychotherapist simply cannot.

The Initial Approach

When I make the first telephone call to a newly assigned client, I think of her as a potential friend and smile while I am speaking. I learned long ago, when doing some telephone solicitation, that a smile is somehow or other communicated over the telephone so that the person on the other end is less likely to view me as a threat and more apt to feel like smiling in return. I try to be casual and relaxed as I ask for directions and set up a mutually convenient appointment.

On my first visit, my aim is to find out as much about my client as I can without appearing too inquisitive. The more completely I can picture the client's situation, the better I will be able to figure out how to help. In return, I try to give her a quick sketch of who I am: where I live, that I am married, that I love animals, and that I enjoy visiting older people. Sometimes, with a talkative client, I am unable to interject all that information, but I try to do so, even if I have to put it that briefly.

During the first visit, I also discuss with the client what we might do together and how often I will be coming to visit—usually once a week. Most of the elders in the companion program are lonely and simply want a bit of company for a few hours, while others would like to go shopping or for a ride. Those in the counseling program are facing some loss in their lives that they need to talk about and work through. Actually, all the elderly in both programs have had losses and are lonely, so although my assignment differs from one program to the other, my attitude and approach are similar.

My clients have all been introduced to me first through a social worker, who has explained my function within the program and let them know that I will see them once a week but that they are not to make frequent if any telephone calls to me. This is done to make certain that a dependent client does not become a daily nuisance to the volunteer. Clarification of my role lets me start to establish a friendship type of relationship from point zero. I can move toward it at my own speed, and that movement is then understood by the client as something personal to her. As indeed it is.

Similarities

I want my client to talk freely to me, to tell me what is on her mind and in her heart, even if it is the same thing every week. To do this, she must feel that I understand what she is saying, that I empathize. Because I am also an older woman (over sixty seems to qualify), I think most clients sense that I have probably felt at least something similar to what they are now feeling. Which is true, at least to some extent, and I am quick both to establish our parity in age and also to find similarities of experience insofar as I can honestly do that.

I am careful, however, never to say, "I know how you feel," because that is rather presumptive and prompts a response, thought if not said, of "Oh no, you don't. You couldn't possibly know how awful it is." Instead, I have found it helpful and in fact more accurate to say something like, "I think I may have some idea of how you feel," followed as possible with a very brief example from my own life, always with the implication that the client's experience is more difficult. Such an approach eliminates competition to see who has the worse problems. I always am brief in anything I tell about myself, because the client needs to talk her problems out, not listen to me. I want simply to let her know that I will be able to understand her feelings because I too have problems, I too am vulnerable.

I also avoid another type of response, which I think of as the "professional" one, largely because it immediately makes me the "counselor" and her the "client," thus dividing me from this person with whom I am hoping to establish a friendship. Examples of the "professional" response, would be "Tell me how you feel about that" or "How did you feel about that?" These responses would be an immediate turnoff to me, and although I might answer, I would take it as a perhaps unintentional clarification of the gulf between counselor and client—a pulling away.

On the other hand, I do use the accepted techniques to make it easier for the client to express her feelings: suggesting words to identify her feelings and re-phrasing what she has told me, to let her know I have understood what she is saying. Insofar as I can, I avoid the word "feel," because of the unease that it elicits from many older people—including me.

A Two-Way Relationship

Another method I have used to put the relationship on a one-to-one friend basis is to try to make it a two-way affair—to ask for my client's interest and understanding of some aspect of my own life. I never do this early in the relationship. And often it is difficult, because she may be so upset or consumed by her own problems that she is unable to consider anyone else at all. Then one can pretend a bit, implying that she has some interest or telling her how fine it is to be able to tell her frankly about something or other. This has worked quite well at times.

An example. I might, at an appropriate moment, say all of a sudden, as if it just popped into my head, "Oh, I have been wanting to tell you about what my horses did yesterday, because I know as a onetime rider you would be interested." Even though I am pretty sure she isn't, really. Usually this approach pushes the client into at least pretending interest and listening. That gives me a few minutes to make her think about someone besides herself, as well as partaking in the exchange more typical of friends than counselor and client. Sometimes I will use a recent snapshot, most often of one of my animals (cats, dogs, horses) rather than family, to set the stage, relying on almost everyone's desire to look at a picture, particularly of an animal.

I try always to avoid seeming like the "lady bountiful" coming to do good to the poor older lady. An amusing observation by Thoreau to this point:

> "If I knew that a man were coming to my house with a conscious design of doing me good, I should run for my life."
>
> [quoted by Bortz, p. 229]

Special Friends

Eventually, most of my clients have seemed to consider me their friend even more than their companion or counselor. This of course has not only increased my responsibility to them, but also my enjoyment of the time spent with them.

It is an old saw that understanding a person leads to liking that person, and I have found this true in most cases. It doesn't mean that on a bad day I am not sometimes bored. I am. But that is true even with friends made outside my elderwork, and mainly it occurs when I am tired or feeling down myself. In other words, the boredom or sometimes irritation has as much to do with me as with my client.

Liking the client, I tell her that I enjoy being with her, sometimes directly and sometimes indirectly. Eventually, she becomes a "special" client, in the same way that all one's children are special. Whichever of my four children I am thinking about at the time feels to me like my very favorite, and I suspect that most mothers resemble me in this. This special status is only implied, partially because I avoid even indirectly criticizing another client, for fear that the present one will wonder if I criticize her also. But I know she feels her specialness. This gives me a real sense of success and helps to solve some of the client's problems in that she knows someone sincerely cares about her and thus feels better about herself.

General Techniques

The very word "techniques" sounds manipulative, an adjective that nowadays has bad connotations. In discussing the relationship that I try to establish, I have already mentioned several techniques, the use of which may sound like a cold and artificial approach to forming a warm bond with another person. I see it rather as a carefully considered way to help someone. Actually, most people perhaps unconsciously use certain techniques to please other people and become friends with them—as, for instance, subtle flattery or expressions of interest in their lives.

With all my clients, the assistance I am trying to give is quite similar and simple. I want to help them handle their losses (such as of mate, home, friends, or mobility) so that they may lead happier lives. The interrelated problems caused by their losses are, to one degree or another, the major three described—loneliness, boredom, and depression. The techniques discussed below are all aimed at relieving one or more of these.

Listening and Conversing

"Active listening" is the phrase most used for the frequently advised technique for companions and counselors. Its importance cannot be overstated, nor can one ever stop checking to be sure that in fact this is what one is doing. It is all too easy to let one's mind drift on hearing the tenth recital of an incident or opinion. The point is to focus absolutely on what the client is talking about, both to understand where she is coming from and what her problems are and also to convince her of your real interest in her and in her problems. Needless to say, it is easiest to listen actively if you really are interested. Which you had better be if you are to do a good job and also enjoy it.

Many older persons because of loneliness will talk nonstop, so that the only task is to guide a client's talk to expressions of her particular unhappiness and also to reminiscences that will give you a fuller picture of her background and personality. The usual conversational skills will do this.

Sometimes, however, one is assigned a client who says little, because of shyness, a natural reticence, or difficulty with the English language. This always means hard work for me. I would much rather guide a boat with a tiller than row it. When I have a shy or reticent client, I use what I call my "weekly list." While driving to my first visit of the week, I find it useful to mentally list possible subjects to talk about in case conversation lags. Subjects include such general ones as the weather and events in my own life in which I am, sometimes ingenuously, assuming her interest. Most of the latter will have a transition from my life to the client's. Examples:

- We had water in the basement last week and did such and such. Has that ever happened to you? When? What solutions have you found?
- Our dog got loose on Monday, and we were terribly worried until she finally returned. We tried this and that. What have you done in those circumstances?

And on to talk about her former pets.

To this list I will be able to add questions based on the past week's conversations with each client. Having the memory of a woman in her sixties, I would never be able to recall those conversations without a way of reminding myself. Despite what I consider my sincere interest in each client, I forget that so and so was to see her doctor on Wednesday, or I wonder if it was Sadie or Elsie with the appointment. I even sometimes confuse the name of the son or daughter of a client with that of another. Such forgetfulness and confusion unfortunately suggest to my client that I do not care much about her, rather than that I also have a good forgetter. On the other hand, my remembering does tell her that I care. And thus I looked for a solution and found one that works for me.

My solution has been to sit down at my computer at the end of a day of visiting and let tumble out whatever I remember about each encounter, in the order that it occurs to me. A half hour will suffice for three or four clients. Usually I find that three clients a day is all I can handle and still do a good job. I never spend any time editing and usually do not even run a spellcheck. Then, when I start out on my next week's visit, I have the printouts of the past week's conversations with me in the car and can look up facts I may have forgotten: the name of the son in Nebraska, when my client will next see her heart specialist, what her primary worry or physical problem was. I am ready to ask appropriate questions about her life, which helps her to know that I do care.

Reminiscing and Holding Up the Mirror

Visitors to older people are usually advised not only to listen actively but also to encourage a client to reminisce. Most people over sixty but particularly over seventy are very willing to do this, probably because most of us, recognizing that we are nearing the end of our lives, are trying—sometimes unconsciously—to bring together all our memories into a coherent whole that will make us feel that we have lived our lives well. We very much want to be able to see ourselves as successful in our own terms, different as they may be, one from another. We are trying to find the meaning of our lives, as discussed earlier.

When a client talks about her past life, she often reveals more than she would wish me to see. I usually can quickly perceive how she wishes to see herself—generous, clever, loving to husband, faithful to friends, financially successful, or wise. Part of my job may be to reflect back to a person what she wishes to see, thus increasing both her self image and also her pleasure in my company. It is my experience that if the picture of herself that I show her is just a bit better than the real one, she will be more successful in becoming like the reflection.

Ruth, for example, is a very religious person who lives alone in a house down the street from her daughter and husband. The daughter is very helpful to Ruth, but Ruth makes it obvious to me that the daughter has many annoying failings. On occasion, however, she will say something that can be construed as praise of her daughter. At such times I will remark on how lucky the young woman is to have a mother that appreciates her so much, because that is not always the case. Seeing herself as generous, I suspect that Ruth is more likely to be so. And thus to be happier herself.

Perceiving a person's weaknesses, I sometimes am tempted to reflect a more accurate picture than she would wish in the hope that she will see herself more clearly and decide to change some of her attitudes. With this approach I have had scant success, having tried upon occasion to sneak it in between more favorable images. I suspect that most older people, somewhere inside them, know their faults and have themselves decided whether or not they wish to change at all.

Chatting and Laughing

A very different client is the one who is so full of fear and despair that the image she would like to see in the mirror is so faint that I cannot distinguish it with certainty. Sadie was one such client. All she showed me were her weaknesses, with which she wanted my help. Although she had emphysema, she smoked a lot and knew it was wrong. She also had, in her words, "sinned" a lot in her life and wanted reassurance that she would not be condemned to hell. She talked of little else but her weaknesses. Finally I realized that she was clinging to her fears and anxieties almost as if they were what gave her her identity. She seemed to feel that if she lost them she would become no one, and everyone who had been trying to help her would leave.

The approach that has been most successful for me with Sadie and other similar clients is to listen carefully, reflect her feelings with a rephrasing, make a suggestion or two, and then talk about something—anything—else. This is when I will start "chatting," telling the client about what happened to me yesterday or perhaps asking what she thinks her town should do about a particular problem recently in the news. I am trying to make her world larger, big enough to include not only me but her neighbors, the city, and the world. In so doing, I may lose her interest, because she lives in a tiny universe, including only herself and perhaps her children. As I see her interest flagging, I return back to her life and try once more to move out from that center.

My major card with this type of client, however, is laughter. Everyone enjoys laughing. Tension is relieved and one feels better after laughing. How this is achieved depends, of course, on the personalities of the two people involved.

The story and picture of this squirrel, rescued from a pond, amused several of the elderly whom the author visits.
—photograph by Brian Wiprud

Possible techniques include kidding, relating amusing incidents, and telling jokes. Not being able to tell jokes very well myself, I rely heavily on the other two approaches.

Sadie responded wonderfully to little stories I told her about my animals and my husband, even remembering to ask me to repeat them the following week. She particularly enjoyed hearing about how one of my sons had rescued a squirrel swimming in a pond by extending an oar to it. The squirrel climbed aboard and rode to shore in the prow of the boat. My son had snapped a picture of the waterlogged squirrel in the boat, and it absolutely delighted Sadie, so I gave her a copy to share with her family.

Rarely do I leave a client without having shared some laughter. I believe laughter makes sessions more enjoyable for us both, leaves the client in a better mood, and makes her look forward to my return the next week. I may overemphasize the importance of this type of fun in a visit, but I think not. I have become aware that a client's laughs with me may well be the only ones she experiences that week. I often judge the success of my visit by how many good laughs the client and I have had.

Professional attention has been paid over the past decade or so to the healing powers of laughter, most notably by Norman Cousins in his *Anatomy of an Illness*. He found that the ancient theory that laughter is good medicine has been confirmed by recent research. Not long ago, I read an article by Scott Badler about The Humor Project and Nurses for Laughter, two organizations dedicated to putting the theory into practice. Joel Goodman, founder of The Humor Project, listed enhanced respiration and circulation, oxygenated blood, and repression of stress-related hormones as some of the benefits.

Offering Suggestions and Answers

Nouwen reminds us that the gift of ourselves and our full attention is more valuable than any suggestions we may offer or deed we may do. He emphasizes the central importance of listening:

> When we are primarily concerned with giving old people something to do, offering them entertainment and distractions, we might avoid the painful realization that most people do not want to be distracted but heard, not entertained but sustained.

[Nouwen, p. 99]

Although I try to concentrate my efforts on listening well to the client, encouraging her to reminisce and bringing a bit of humor and the outside world into her life, there are times when it seems appropriate to make a few concrete suggestions. Doing so is a tricky business. I use the term "suggestions" rather than "advice," because I am careful not to advise. I want my client to believe, insofar as possible, that she has come up with a solution, or, failing that, that we have come up with it together. Like people of any age, she is more likely to implement the suggestion if it is not laid upon her, particularly by someone younger than she.

Most of my suggestions are, of course, those already listed earlier, with the descriptions of Mildred and Lucille, for coping with the three bugaboos of loneliness, boredom, and depression. I simply tailor them to the particular client and make them specific to her situation.

An even trickier business is answering the difficult questions that a client may put to a sympathetic visitor. I refer to questions such as Sadie's, when she asked, "Will God send me to Hell for all the bad things I did when I was younger?" Lucille also asked that question again and again. Another daunting and more frequent one is, "Why doesn't God 'take' me, why does He make me live on, unhappy and in pain as I am? I am useless to everyone and a nuisance to many. Why does he let me live?" This is a frequent question, particularly from Jane.

My instinctive—and I think wise—reaction is to duck the question. I usually try to keep the client talking, leading her to say what she is thinking about or feeling. After all, most of the time she doesn't really expect or even want me to answer her question. She doesn't think that I know more about her concern than she does, particularly since I am younger than she.

However, sometimes the question is put so forcefully and repeatedly that I feel some sort of an answer is clearly wanted. In such situations I cannot resist attempting a response. The first part of my answer is always that I really don't know. If she persists, I will move on to an answer of sorts, always putting it in a personal context: "This is the way it seems to me when I ask myself the question. Maybe it will help."

In response to both questions, I rely on a very homely simile that has meaning for me. I could, of course, point to the book of Job, where it is made abundantly clear that God is great and all-powerful, and that man cannot possibly understand His ways. Instead of calling on the Bible, however, I ask my client to consider for a moment the relationship of herself and her dog, or some animal she has once owned and loved. I compare this to God's relationship to her—the one all-powerful and loving to the other, while the other cannot understand many of the actions of the powerful and loving one.

To an older client whose fear of death focuses on conviction that God will punish her after death for her sins, real or imagined, I ask what she would do to her beloved little dog or cat if it soiled the rug or didn't come when called. Would she punish it by chiding it and smacking its rear end, or would she torture it in hellfire? Obviously not the latter. Then I ask her to remember that God's love for even his very disobedient children is much greater than our love for our disobedient pets. So how could she imagine that God would torture his children in hellfire?

When asked the other question—why God allows or forces her to live beyond her usefulness and possibly in pain—I simply ask her if the dog understands why he must spend a day penned in the kitchen when she is away. And then I point out that she knows why this is necessary but the dog, being only a dog, cannot. Even so with God. He has a reason that we, being only human, cannot know, but we can be sure that whatever He is doing is best.

I cannot tell how helpful my responses have been when I have had to give them, but at least I have been honest and presented a picture that may stay with a person simply because it is a bit different and from real life.

Fortunately, I do not often have to tackle these difficult questions. I focus on using the techniques outlined above, coming up with practical solutions to specific daily problems when required, and remaining aware that my basic purpose in visiting is to channel God's caring love to each person. I often show affection, sometimes with a hug (only for those who welcome it and not too early in a relationship), other times with a pressure of the hand, and more often just with facial expressions that show the client that I enjoy being with her. Nothing is more effective than smiling. I cannot solve my client's deeper problems, but I can help her know how special she is. Even if she has been more content only during the hour or two of my visit, my time has been well spent. And if over the weeks she retains after my visits some awareness that she is special (to God, if she believes—which most do, to some extent—or at least to me), this is the biggest reward of all.

However, I would like to do more. One time, Jane—who is especially dear to me—asked me, "Why does God let me live? I am of no use to anyone. I always helped others, and now they must help me. Of what use am I?" She had expressed this feeling several times before, and I had used up my "I don't know" and "we cannot understand God's ways" responses. I was yearning to say to her, "God wants you now to just *be*, not *do*." She is a religious woman who reads her Bible every day. I figured she just might understand. So I said it, drew a blank, and then tried to resay it in all sorts of ways. She had no idea what I was talking about. She knew I was trying to be helpful and was failing in the attempt, so she politely turned our conversation to something else.

The incident had a replay. I had another chance, and this time I did better. I didn't try to speak in the spiritual, philosophic language that happens to be meaningful to me. Instead, I translated to another language that had meaning for her. I simply told her that she is useful, but that she just doesn't know it. I explained to her how her wisdom had helped me, how loved I felt by her, and how much pleasure her company always gives me. I said that it wasn't merely her tea and cookies I enjoyed, but also her stories about her life, her friendship, and just the way she was. She seemed to understand. She smiled across the table at me and seemed filled. I had learned something important.

Nouwen suggests that our loving and respectful attitude toward an older person will help provide the sense of self-worth that people need who are facing the challenges of old age.

> Quite often our concern to preach, teach, or cure prevents us from perceiving and receiving what those we care for have to offer. Does not healing, first of all, take place by the restoration of a sense of self-worth? But how can that take place unless there is someone able to discover the beauty of the other and willing to receive it as a precious gift? Where else do we realize that we are valuable people except in the eyes of those who by their care affirm our own best self?
>
> [Nouwen, p. 95]

Our time, our minds, our full attention, and finally our empathy and our love. "All else will follow as the night the day."

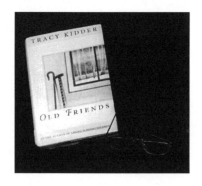

Annotated Bibliography

Collections

Booth, Wayne. *The Art of Growing Older: Writers on Living and Aging.* Chicago: The University of Chicago Press, 1996. First published in 1992. 336 pp.
A collection of poetry and poetic prose about aging, much of it by older poets, interspersed by literary, amusing, and perceptive comments by the author/editor. Booth, Professor of English Emeritus at the University of Chicago, was seventy-one at the time of writing.

Cole, Thomas R. and Mary G. Winkler, eds. *The Oxford Book of Aging: Reflections on the Journey of Life.* New York: Oxford University Press, 1994. 419 pp.
A comprehensive volume of 250 pieces about aging of all genres, "across the boundaries of time, race, culture, ethnicity, and gender," organized around nine themes.

Fowler, Margaret and Priscilla McCutcheon, eds. *Songs of Experience: An Anthology of Literature on Growing Old.* New York: Ballantine Books, 1991. 379 pp.
Memoirs and musings by twentieth century writers on growing old. Excellent. This is the book I would recommend if only one were chosen for further reading.

Martz, Sandra Haldeman, ed. *Grow Old Along With Me; The Best is Yet to Be.* Watsonville, California: Papier-Mâché Press, 1996. 187 pp.
A selection of poems, stories, and photographs by men and women fifty years old and above about growing older.

_____. *When I Am an Old Woman I Shall Wear Purple.* Watsonville, California: Papier-Mâché Press, 1987.
A selection of poems, stories, and photographs by women of all ages about growing older.

Interviews

Berman, Phillip L. and Connie Goldman. *The Ageless Spirit.* New York: Ballantine Books, 1992. 282 pp.

A collection of forty essays based on interviews with a diverse group of creative people over seventy years old by Connie Goldman. The interviews were used for a National Public Radio series in the mid 1980s.

Blythe, Ronald. *The View in Winter.* New York: Penguin Books, 1981. First published by Allen Lane, 1979. 319 pp.

Interviews with thirty-nine British men and women over fifty speaking of their experiences with their own and others' aging.

Erikson, Erik H., Joan M. and Helen Q. Kivnick. *Vital Involvement in Old Age.* New York: W. W. Norton & Co., 1986. 350 pp.

Joint reflections on the coping strategies in old age, based on interviews with twenty-nine octogenarians. The emphasis is on the effectiveness of being vitally involved in life.

Kidder, Tracy. *Old Friends.* New York: Houghton Mifflin, 1993. 352 pp.

The engrossing story of the friendship and development of two nursing home residents. Based on a year spent by the author in a Northampton nursing home, it shows that life at its best and most interesting is still possible. Amusing, touching, and perceptive.

York, Pat. *Going Strong: Portraits and Interviews with Seventy People Seventy-Five and Older—Still Going Strong.* New York: Arcade Publishing, Inc., 1991. 255 pp.

Responses to a questionnaire by people over seventy-five who had not retired and were contributing notably to society. Color photographs of each.

Autobiographies and Journals

Cousins, Norman. *Anatomy of an Illness.* New York: W. W. Norton & Co., 1970. 173 pp.

The story of the author's fight against a crippling disease, using laughter, courage, and the powers of mind and spirit.

_____. *Healing Heart.* New York: W. W. Norton & Co., 1970. 288 pp.

The story of the author's massive heart attack. It emphasizes the patient's role in combating serious illness in close partnership with his physician.

Fisher, M. F. K. *Last House: Reflections, Dreams, and Observations, 1943-1991.* Pantheon Books, 1995. 289 pp.

A collection of short pieces written between thirty-eight and eighty-six years of age, a few concerning how she feels in her final years. Fisher is best known for her witty and erudite books about dining and cooking.

Goudeket, Maurice. *The Delights of Growing Old.* Patrick O'Brian, translator. Pleasantville, New York: The Akadine Press, 1996. First published in French in 1965. 214 pp.

An amusing autobiography written at the age of seventy-five that emphasizes the joys of aging. Maurice Goudeket was the husband of the French novelist and essayist Colette.

Grumbach, Doris. *Coming into the End Zone: A Memoir.* New York: W. W. Norton & Co., 1991.

This "candid, moving, and flinty journal" of her seventieth year is interesting, but not as deep as May Sarton's. Novelist Grumbach was literary editor of *The New Republic* and a regular book reviewer for National Public Radio.

Rose, Xenia. *Widow's Journey: A Return to the Loving Self.* New York: Henry Holt & Co., 1990. 205 pp.

The autobiographical story of Leonard Rose's wife's recovery after his death, including stories about other widows.

Sarton, May.

These ten journals, written between the ages of fifty-six and eighty-two, are increasingly concerned with the challenges of aging and approaching death.

Their main subject, however, is Sarton's struggle to achieve excellence and recognition as a poet and novelist. They were published as paperbacks by W. W. Norton & Co. New York, and are listed in the order of their writing.

Plant Dreaming Deep. 1968. Paperback, 1983. 189 pp.
Journal of a Solitude. 1973. Paperback, 1977. 208 pp.
A World of Light: Portraits and Celebrations. 1976. Paperback, 1988. 252 pp.
The House by the Sea. 1977. Paperback, 1981. 286 pp.
Recovering: A Journal. 1980. Paperback, 1986. 246 pp.
At Seventy: A Journal. 1984. Paperback, 1987. 334 pp.
After the Stroke. A Journal. 1984. Paperback, 1990. 280 pp.
Endgame: A Journal of the Seventy-Ninth Year. 1992. Paperback, 1995. 345 pp.
Encore: A Journal of the Eightieth Year. 1993. Paperback, 1995. 332 pp.
At Eighty-Two: A Journal. 1996. Paperback, 1997. 350 pp.

Scott-Maxwell, Florida. *The Measure of My Days.* New York: Penguin Books, 1979. First published in the USA by Alfred A. Knopf, Inc., 1968. 150 pp.

Diffuse but perceptive journal entries concerning old age, written in Scott-Maxwell's eighties. She was a playwright and practicing Jungian analyst.

Vining, Elizabeth Gray. *Being Seventy: The Measure of a Year.* New York: The Viking Press, 1978. 194 pp.

A journal describing Vining's experiences in her seventieth year (1972), including a visit to Japan, and her thoughts about aging. Very well written. Vining wrote stories for children and adults, a book about her experiences as the tutor for Japan's Crown Prince (1946-50), and an autobiography.

Discussions of Aging

Bortz, Dr. Walter M., II. *We Live Too Short and Die Too Long: How to Achieve and Enjoy Your Natural 100-Year-Plus Life Span.* New York: Bantam Books, 1991. 296 pp.

A guide to aging by a leading authority on the subject. Dr. Bortz develops the thesis that the human body is meant to last 120 years, and then sets out the essential, controllable elements of longevity and specific ways to achieve a longer, more active life and a quick death. Very well-written, with many descriptions of long-lived individuals.

Boyd, Malcolm. *Rich With Years: Daily Meditations on Growing Older.* New York: HarperCollins Publishers, 1993.

Informal essays headed by quotes that spark them. Of the type one finds in a daily newspaper. Boyd is an Episcopal priest and writes a column for *Modern Maturity.*

Cowley, Malcolm. *The View From 80.* New York: The Viking Press, 1980. 74 pp.

Expansion of an article in *Life* containing many quotes about aging, making a distinction between those by people over eighty and those younger. Perceptive, sensitive. Includes the poem, "The Red Wagon."

Downs, Hugh. *Fifty to Forever.* Nashville, Tennessee: Thomas Nelson, Inc., 1994. 342 pp.

A source of practical information to prepare older adults and their families for the choices they may have to make. Includes information on aging, attitudes, post-retirement employment, health, the role of the family, housing options, dementia, and nursing homes.

Friedan, Betty. *The Fountain of Age.* New York: Simon & Schuster, 1993. 671 pp.

Heavy with research on the mystique of aging, this tome includes many examples of successful aging. The emphasis is on aging as an adventure, with new possibilities of intimacy and purpose rather than decline in the "Third Age." Friedan is best known as a feminist author and speaker.

Hallowell, Christopher. *Growing Old, Staying Young.* New York: William Morrow & Co., 1985. 301 pp.

A well-written discussion of how to grow old, including recommendations on attitude, Alzheimer's, retirement, as well as detailed discussion of exercise and diet. Hallowell is a medical doctor and science writer whose language is clear and who provides many good definitions in the text as well as in the glossary.

Harton, Sibyl. *On Growing Old: A Preparation for Age.* New York: Morehouse-Gorham Co. 1957. 126 pp.

A religious approach to aging. Harton, the wife of a British clergyman, provides a very spiritual approach to loneliness, uselessness, dependence, and other problems of the very old. Written in an informal, quaint, and discursive style.

Kroll, Una. *Growing Older.* London: Fount Paperbacks. 1988. 224 pp.
A positive discussion of aging by a well-known British counselor and writer who is also a doctor and deaconess. It offers chapters on aging's pleasures, its problems, physical threats, and advice for the "journey."

Kubler-Ross, Elisabeth. *On Death and Dying.* New York: Macmillan Publishing Co., Inc., 1969. 289 pp.
A classic on the subject of dying. It defines the stages of dying as denial, anger, depression, bargaining, and acceptance, while emphasizing the necessity for hope. Kubler-Ross is a medical doctor whose interviews with many of her dying patients form the core of her book. Warm and sensitive.

LeShan, Eda. *Oh, To Be 50 Again.* New York: Times Books, 1986. 370 pp.
A candid, perceptive, and amusing discussion of aging by a sixty-three-year-old, with emphasis on "the never-ending search for oneself." She discusses illness, marriage, grown children, grandchildren, aged parents, widowhood, and dying. Includes many examples from interviews. LeShan is a noted educator, family counselor, and columnist for *Newsday.*

_____. *It's Better to Be Over the Hill Than Under It.* New York: Newmarket Press, 1990. 227 pp.
Similar to *Oh, To Be 50 Again,* this collection of essays discusses many of the same topics, but from the perspective of an older woman (sixty-seven) who has suffered a stroke during the past year. The emphasis is on accepting old age and bringing "meaning into our lives by our own creativity and what we can do for others."

Linkletter, Art. *Old Age Is Not For Sissies.* New York: Viking Penguin Inc., 1988. 352 pp.
A source of practical information about choices in housing, health care, financial security, abuse, and lifestyle for seniors.

Nouwen, Henri J. M. and Walter J. Gaffney. *Aging.* Garden City, New York: Doubleday & Co., Inc. 1974. 152 pp.
A diffuse discussion of aging and caring for the aged by a Dutch priest-psychologist and a Connecticut community worker. With many photographs. There are some interesting remarks about the relationship of the caregiver with the care receiver.

Nuland, Sherwin B. *How We Die: Reflections on Life's Final Chapter.* New York: Random House, 1995. 278 pp.
A compassionate but unblinking and detailed description by a surgeon of deaths from cancer, heart attack, stroke, AIDS, and Alzheimer's disease. He tries to dispel the myth of dignified death, while suggesting that dignity must be in the life preceding it. This powerful and well written book gives lively descriptions of many individuals' dying and death.

Pollin, Irene and Susan Golant. *Taking Charge: Overcoming the Challenges of Long-Term Illness.* New York: Random House, 1994. 262 pp.

Step-by-step guide of practical advice for dealing with the current medical care system and the emotional challenges of a final illness. Compassionate and clear, but over-organized and repetitive.

Skinner, B. F. and M. E. Vaughan. *Enjoy Old Age.* New York: W. W. Norton & Co., Inc., 1983.

Practical advice for handling all the small and large inconveniences of old age. Written at the age of seventy-nine by Skinner, with Vaughan's help, this quaint and very plainly written little book also discusses attitudes toward old age and provides a quilt of quotes and near quotes, obviously as they jumped into Skinner's mind while writing. Skinner at that time was professor emeritus of psychology at Harvard, where Vaughan was a research associate.

Fiction

Berry, Wendell. *The Memory of Old Jack.* New York: Harcourt Brace Jovanich, Inc., 1974. 223 pp.

An aged and much respected Kentucky farmer remembers his life in the fields and with his family and neighbors. Old Jack's musings might seem like senility.

Ellis, Alice Thomas. *The Summer House.* New York: Penguin Books, 1994. First published in the United Kingdom, 1987. 339 pp.

In the second story in this trilogy, titled "The Skeleton in the Cupboard," an old woman tells her version of the same story that is told in the other two parts and describes how it feels to be old.

Fisher, M. F. K. *Sister Age.* New York: Alfred A. Knopf, Inc. 1983. 243 pp.

A collection of arresting and odd stories about older people. M. F. K. Fisher is primarily known for her books about food.

Godwin, Gail. *The Good Husband.* New York: Ballantine Books, 1994. 468 pp.

The story focuses on Magda Danvers' dying and death from cancer, her relationship with her husband during that period, and the effect that she has on several close friends as she is dying. An academic setting. Very perceptive.

Lester, Julius. *Do Lord Remember Me.* New York: Holt, Rinehart and Winston, 1984. 210 pp.

Reverend Joshua Smith tells the story of his last few days, with his memories and musings about his life as a black minister before the civil rights movement. He illustrates the spiritual growth that can come from remembering at the end of life.

Novick, Marian. *At Her Age.* New York: Charles Scribner's Sons, 1985. 258 pp.

"Intrepid" Molly leaves a nursing home for a fling in New York, and eventually is reconciled with her daughter and grandchildren. Zany, witty, moving.

Sarton, May. *As We Are Now.* New York: W. W. Norton & Co., 1973. Paperback, 1982. 134 pp.

A seventy-six-year-old retired schoolteacher, mentally strong but physically frail, is placed in a nursing home, leading to a surprise but psychologically sound and harrowing denouement. Sarton is the author of poetry and journals as well as novels.

———. *Kinds of Love.* 1970. New York: W. W. Norton & Co., 1970. Paperback, 1980. 464 pp.

An older couple who summer in Willard learn more about their various love-friendship relationships there and develop a more mature bond with each other.

Stegner, Wallace. *Angle of Repose.* New York: Doubleday & Company, 1971. (New York: Penguin Books, 1992). 569 pp.

A retired historian, confined to a wheelchair, writes his grandparents' story as he comes to terms with his own life. Stegner is a prize-winning author who taught writing at various major universities.

Sources

The first three parts of this section provide full bibliographical information for the abbreviated citations in brackets at the end of each quotation within the text. When only one book or article by an author has been cited, no title is given in the brackets. When more than one book by an author has been cited, the book's title is given in abbreviated form. In many instances, an author's work comes from one of three collections, abbreviated in the text as *Ageless, Oxford,* and *Songs.* The fourth part of this section credits persons interviewed for this book.

Books

Berman, Phillip L. and Connie Goldman. *The Ageless Spirit.* New York: Ballantine Books, 1992.

Berry, Wendell. *The Memory of Old Jack.* New York: Harcourt Brace Jovanich, Inc., 1974.

Booth, Wayne. *The Art of Growing Older: Writers on Living and Aging.* Chicago: The University of Chicago Press, 1996. First published in 1992.

Bortz, Dr. Walter M., II. *We Live Too Short and Die Too Long: How to Achieve and Enjoy Your Natural 100-Year-Plus Life Span.* New York: Bantam Books, 1991.

Boyd, Malcolm. *Rich With Years: Daily Meditations on Growing Older.* New York: HarperCollins Publishers, 1993.

Cole, Thomas R. and Mary G. Winkler. *The Oxford Book of Aging: Reflections on the Journey of Life.* New York: Oxford University Press, 1994.

Cowley, Malcolm. *The View From 80.* New York: The Viking Press, 1980.

Ellis, Alice Thomas. *The Summer House.* New York: Penguin Books, 1994. First published in the United Kingdom in 1987.

Fisher, M. F. K. *Last House: Reflections, Dreams, and Observations, 1943-1991.* New York: Pantheon Books, 1995.

_____. *Sister Age.* New York: Alfred A. Knopf, Inc., 1983.

Fowler, Margaret and Priscilla McCutcheon, eds. *Songs of Experience: An Anthology of Literature on Growing Old*. New York: Ballantine Books, 1991.

Friedan, Betty. *The Fountain of Age*. New York: Simon & Schuster, 1993.

Godwin, Gail. *The Good Husband*. New York: Ballantine Books, 1994.

Goudeket, Maurice. *The Delights of Growing Old*. Patrick O'Brian, translator. Pleasantville, New York: The Akadine Press, 1996. First published in French in 1965.

Hallowell, Christopher. *Growing Old, Staying Young.* New York: William Morrow & Co., Inc., 1985.

Harton, Sibyl. *On Growing Old: A Preparation for Age*. New York: Morehouse-Gorham Co., 1957.

Kubler-Ross, Elisabeth. *On Death and Dying*. New York: Macmillan Publishing Co., Inc., 1969.

LeShan, Eda. *Oh, To Be 50 Again*. New York: Times Books, 1986.

_____. *It's Better to Be Over the Hill Than Under It*. New York: Newmarket Press, 1990.

Lester, Julius. *Do Lord Remember Me*. New York: Holt, Rinehart and Winston, 1984.

Nouwen, Henri J. M. and Gaffney, Walter J. *Aging*, Garden City, New York: Doubleday & Co., Inc., 1974.

Nuland, Sherwin B. *How We Die: Reflections on Life's Final Chapter*. New York: Vintage Books, 1995. First published by Alfred A. Knopf, Inc., 1994.

Sarton, May. New York: W. W. Norton & Co.

_____. *Plant Dreaming Deep*. 1968. Paperback, 1983.

_____. *Kinds of Love*. Paperback, 1970. Paperback, 1980.

_____. *At Seventy: A Journal*. 1984. Paperback, 1987.

_____. *Endgame: A Journal of the Seventy-Ninth Year*. 1992. Paperback, 1995.

_____. *Encore: A Journal of the Eightieth Year*. 1993. Paperback, 1995.

_____. *At Eighty-Two: A Journal*. 1996. Paperback, 1997.

Scott-Maxwell, Florida. *The Measure of My Days*. New York: Penguin Books, 1979. First published in the U. S. A. by Alfred A. Knopf, Inc., 1968.

Skinner, B. F. and M. E. Vaughan. *Enjoy Old Age*. New York: W. W. Norton & Co., Inc., 1983.

Vining, Elizabeth Gray. *Being Seventy: The Measure of a Year*. New York: The Viking Press, 1978.

Articles

Batten, Mary. "Take Charge of Pain," *Modern Maturity*, January-February 1995. pp. 35-37, 80-81.

Friedan, Betty. "How To Live Longer, Better, Wiser," *Parade Magazine*, March 20, 1994. pp. 4-6.

_____. "My Quest for the Fountain of Age," *Time*, September 6, 1993. pp. 61-64

Jacobson, Stanley. "Overselling Depression to the Old Folks," *The Atlantic Monthly*, April, 1995. pp. 46-51.

Lauerman, John. "Toward a Natural History of Aging," *Harvard Magazine*, September-October, 1996. pp. 57-65.

Smith, Lee. "The Happy Memories Club," *The Atlantic Monthly*, December, 1995. pp. 8-18.

Collections

The Ageless Spirit. Phillip L. Berman and Connie Goldman, eds. New York: Ballantine Books, 1992. Pieces were written by the following individual authors for *The Ageless Spirit:*

Eddie Albert	Art Linkletter
Phillip Berman	Rollo May
Ossie Davis	Eve Merriam
Maggie Kuhn	Jason Robards, Jr.
Stanley Kunitz	Arthur M. Schlesinger, Jr.
George Leonard	Beatrice Wood
Bella Lewitzky	

Oxford Book of Aging: Reflections on the Journey of Life. Thomas R. Cole and Mary G. Winkler, eds. New York: Oxford University Press, 1994.

ben Shea, Noah. From "Reality Rides the Current," in *Jacob the Baker*, 1989.

Burns, Olive Ann. From *Cold Sassy Tree*.

Butler, Robert N. From "The Life Review: An Interpretation of Reminiscence in the Aged," 1963.

Hesse, Hermann. From "On Old Age," in *My Belief: Essays on Life and Art*. 1952.

Le Sueur, Meridel. Remarks preceding a poem entitled, "Rites of Ancient Ripening." 1986.

Myerhoff, Barbara G. From "Re-membered Lives." 1980.

Newton, Ellen. From "This Bed My Centre." 1979.

Russell, Bertrand. "Pros and Cons of Reaching Ninety." 1962.

Toynbee, Arnold. From "Janus at Seventy-Five (14 April 1964)." in *Experiences*, 1969.

Twain, Mark. From an address given at a dinner in New York City on December 5, 1905.

Williams, Carter Catlett. From "Salsify and Sacrament." 1993.

Songs of Experience: An Anthology of Literature on Growing Old. Margaret Fowler and Priscilla McCutcheon, eds. New York: Ballantine Books, 1991. Including the following selections:

Berenson, Bernard. From "Sunset and Twilight: Diaries of 1947-1958."

Brecht, Bertolt. From "Everything Changes."

Coatsworth, Elizabeth. Foreword from "Personal Geography: Almost an Autobiography."

Francis, Polly. "The Autumn of My Life." The complete first article of three.

Glasgow, Ellen. From "The Woman Within."

Hayes, Helen. From "Voices: An Epilogue."

Larkin, Philip. From "Aubade."

Lindbergh, Anne Morrow. From a 1983 speech.

Roosevelt, Eleanor. From an interview, excerpted from *This I Believe,* by Edward P. Morgan, ed.

Stark, Freya. From "The Journey's Echo."

Van Duyn, Mona. From "Letters from a Father."

Persons Interviewed

The following persons graciously agreed to be interviewed for this book and to allow their names to be given. They have approved the text about them and given permission for their pictures to be published. All but one of the many clients whose experiences in aging provided a major source of information are not named, to preserve their privacy and to respect the confidentiality assured by the agencies for whom the author was volunteering as counselor or companion. The exception is

Mildred Crossman of Bernardston, who gave the same approval and permission as those interviewed.

Elsa Bakalar on Monday, February 23, 1998, at 10:30 A.M. at her winter home in Ashfield, Massachusetts.

Grace Blanchard on Monday, February 23, 1998, at 2 P.M. at her home in Greenfield, Massachusetts.

Arline Cohn on Saturday, February 21, 1998, at 10:30 A.M. at her home in Greenfield, Massachusetts.

Barbara Sleigh Ellis on Monday, February 2, 1998, at 2 P.M. at her home in Athol, Massachusetts.

Annabelle and Robert Haven on Friday, February 13, 1998, at 4 P.M. at their home in Athol, Massachusetts.

Alice and Burt Newton on Friday, February 27, 1998, at 10 A.M. at their home in Athol, Massachusetts.

Charlotte Prince Ryan on Sunday, February 15, 1998, at 2 P.M. at her home in North Orange, Massachusetts.

Credits

About the Author

Helen Hills was born Helen Kerst Runyeon in Reading, Pennsylvania, on December 9, 1929, one half hour after the arrival of her fraternal twin, Mary. They both attended Baldwin School in Bryn Mawr, Pennsylvania, for their last two years of secondary school and then went on to Wellesley College, where they majored in English literature. Helen married at the end of her junior year, becoming Mrs. Grant W. Wiprud. She returned to Wellesley in the fall and graduated with honors the following June.

As Helen Wiprud, she and her husband lived in the Washington, D.C., area and had four children within an eight-year period: Valerie, Rebecca, Ted, and Brian. Enlarging her life only occasionally with painting and horseback riding, Helen was a full-time mother until her youngest entered school. Subsequently, she spent twenty-five years as an employee of the U.S. Government, utilizing her writing skills in various positions, primarily with the U.S. Department of Education. During this time, she and her husband divorced, and she lived alone for fifteen years. She also acquired two horses, two dogs, and two cats.

In early 1991, musician Ralph Hills came into Helen's life and they married in September of the same year. The following April Helen retired, and in May she and her new husband moved with their animal menagerie up to the small town of Warwick in north central Massachusetts. Very soon Helen became a volunteer in the two Franklin County programs for the elderly that are described in her book.

At present, Helen continues in her volunteer efforts and also writes a weekly column entitled "I've Been Thinking About—" for a local newspaper.

For relaxation and sociability, she rides horseback on nearby trails with friends whenever the weather permits, which means from late April, when the deep mud usually dries out, until mid-December, when the first snow turns into ice underfoot. Other times, Helen and her husband enjoy hiking with the dogs, clearing trails, biking, and cross-country skiing. Evenings usually find them both engrossed in reading. Occasional visits from faraway children and grandchildren, as well as relatives and friends, upset the routine delightfully.

Having written this book about aging, Helen is determined to live well into her nineties so that she can make full use of her research.

The author demonstrates the technique of separating eggs to her granddaughter Allegra, above.

—photograph by Kim Lovejoy

Index